GOLD *of* GREECE

Jewelry and Ornaments from the Benaki Museum

The Dallas showing of GOLD OF GREECE *and this catalogue are supported by a grant from Corrigan's Jewelers.*

GOLD *of* GREECE

Jewelry and Ornaments from the Benaki Museum

Revised Text

ANNE R. BROMBERG

Photography

MAKIS SKIADARESSIS

DALLAS MUSEUM OF ART

Gold of Greece: Jewelry and Ornaments from the Benaki Museum
This exhibition was organized by the Benaki Museum, Athens, and the Dallas Museum
of Art. The exhibition is supported by an indemnity from the Federal Council on the
Arts and the Humanities. The official carriers of the exhibition are American Airlines
and Olympic Airways who have generously provided transportation of personnel and
works of art.

**The Dallas showing of *Gold of Greece* and this catalogue are supported by a
grant from Corrigan's Jewelers.**

FRONT COVER
One of a pair of sphinxes
ARCHAIC PERIOD

FRONTISPIECE
Oak wreath
ROMAN PERIOD

BACK COVER
*Medallion with bust
of Aphrodite*
HELLENISTIC PERIOD

DALLAS MUSEUM OF ART
April 8 - June 10, 1990

COOPER-HEWITT MUSEUM, THE SMITHSONIAN INSTITUTION'S
NATIONAL MUSEUM OF DESIGN
September 11, 1990 - January 13, 1991

SAN DIEGO MUSEUM OF ART
February 16 - March 31, 1991

FINE ARTS MUSEUMS OF SAN FRANCISCO
April 27 - June 30, 1991

LIBRARY OF CONGRESS CATALOG CARD NUMBER
90-80359
ISBN 0-936227-07-9 softcover (Dallas Museum of Art)

Editor
Robert V. Rozelle

Manuscript
Linda Ledford

Design and art
Tom Dawson and Bill Maize
DUO Design Group
Fort Worth

Separations
JTM Colorscan, Inc.
Fort Worth

Typography
Lino Typographers, Inc.
Fort Worth

Printing
Hurst Printing Company
Dallas

ACKNOWLEDGMENTS

This publication, *Gold of Greece: Jewelry and Ornaments from the Benaki Museum*, was created on the occasion
of a travelling exhibition that first opened at the Dallas Museum of Art in April 1990. The exhibition catalogue,
however, is based in large part on materials created by the staff of the Benaki Museum of Athens, Greece, and an
international team of experts who authored, photographed and contributed materials for the present exhibition and
its catalogue, as well as for a major publication now in production that will bring world-wide attention to the Benaki
Museum's incomparable permanent collection of Greek jewelry and ornaments. It is to the following members of
the Benaki Museum Exhibition and Catalogue Team that this publication is dedicated:

Authors Anna Ballian, Christos Boulotis, David Buckton, Angelos Delivorrias, Electra Georgoula, Imma Kilian-
Dirlmeier, Stamatis Lymperopoulos, Cyril Mango, Katerina Meletakou, Stella G. Miller, Andrew Oliver, Jr.,
Semeli Pingiatoglou, Elizabeth-Bettina Tsigarida, Athanasios N. Vildirides, Aimilia Yeroulanou.

Editorial Coordinator Electra Georgoula *Assistants* Kate Synodinou, Pitsa Tsakona and Irini Yeroulanou.

Photography Makis Skiadaressis.

English Translations Timothy Cullen, Alex Doumas, David Hardy, John Leatham, Judith Perlzweig-Binder, Kay
Tsitseli-Palaiologou, and David Turner.

Exhibits Supervisor Youla Riska *Conservators* Emilia Kossona and Justin Lee.

Financial Administrator Maria Apostolopoulou.

CONTENTS

PREFACE

In an age in which jewelry and other "gold" ornaments are so common as to be commonplace, it is almost impossible to imagine the sheer luxury and preciousness that belonged to a simple gold ring in ancient Mycenaean civilization or a necklace in Classical Athens. Yet, even to eyes that have suffered a glut of slick Madison Avenue ads, of "costume" jewelry, and of gold chains on Hollywood stars, the jewelry and ornaments from the Benaki Museum in *Gold of Greece* are splendid indeed. From them we learn that the technical wizardry of Greek goldsmiths has scarcely been equalled in our age of machines, vacuum molds, and plastic adhesives. The vaunted technology of the 20th century may have cured dread diseases, raised the standard of living, sent satellites to orbit the earth and men to the moon, but it has not wrought gold with any greater delicacy and subtlety than that known centuries ago in Greece.

The history of the *Gold of Greece* exhibition is as rich in collaboration and exchange as the gold itself is in historical—and monetary—value. It began many years ago when then DMA Director Harry Parker worked with colleagues at the Benaki Museum to create an exhibition about the Athens Museum. This project, like many wonderful exchanges, was delayed temporarily, and then was taken up again by Virginia Nick of Dallas and Angelos Delivorrias and Spyros Mercouris of Athens. I feel fortunate to have arrived at that time and to have had an opportunity to participate in the plans for this show.

The richness of the Benaki collections is indescribable to someone who has never seen them. Indeed, if one could conjure an image of the vast collections of the Victoria and Albert Museum crammed into a 19th-century house in Athens, it would give some indication of the concentrated richness, variety, and sheer life in the Benaki Museum. Like many great institutions, it reflects the ideology of its private founder, Anthony Benaki. Unlike others, Benaki realized that works of art speak more powerfully than words, and he chose to demonstrate this by establishing a museum in which all the civilizations of Hellenism—whether archaic, classical, Roman, or Byzantine—are united under one roof.

It became clear to both Angelos Delivorrias and myself on our first joint tour of the museum that the medium that best linked these various cultural expressions was "gold." Whether beaten into the simple shapes of geometric jewelry or "drawn" in filigree patterns by Post-Byzantine Greeks, gold persists through all the cultures, the religions, and the politics of Greece throughout the ages. And, in viewing the exhibition, we can see not only master-pieces of the jeweler's art, but also the steadfast cultural integrity of the Greeks themselves.

Since Harry Parker was the "godfather" of this project, we are happy that the exhibition will travel to San Francisco for a sort of reunion. There is also a "goddess" of the exhibition, Virginia Nick, a private citizen of Dallas, whose enthusiasm for Greece is boundless. Without her triumphant spirit and tenacity, there would have been no *Gold of Greece*. There have been so many memorable friendships and collegial relationships spawned by the exhibition that they, more than any acknowledgements, will be proof of the exhibition's success as an international collaboration between the modern city of Dallas and the ancient city of Athens.

The most heartfelt of thanks goes to Spyros Mercouris, who as an advisor helped to expedite the official governmental matters with a very cooperative and supportive Greek Ministry of Culture. Afterwards, the brilliant staff of the Benaki Museum, headed by its director Angelos Delivorrias and administrative project coordinator, Mrs. Electra Georgoula, joined with the Dallas Museum family to finalize details of the exhibition and to ensure that its installation and presentation be executed in a quality manner.

The staff of the DMA have all worked on *Gold of Greece* in some capacity, but certain individuals deserve special recognition. Former staff member Jack Rutland was actively involved in the early stages of organizing the exhibition. Barney Delabano, our Exhibition Designer, made a belated first trip to Athens in preparation for the DMA showing of the Benaki collection, and none of us are likely to forget listening to him recount his experience of sightseeing the ancient and charming capital of Athens. Robert Rozelle edited the publication and coordinated its production, while Tom Dawson and Bill Maize created the elegant design, and JTM Colorscan and Hurst Printing combined to produce the beautiful book. Associate Registrar Steve Mann supervised the packing and shipping arrangements for the exhibition, while Judy Nix, Director of Development, vigorously pursued support for the Dallas showing. Anne Bromberg, the DMA Curator of *The Gold of Three Continents* exhibition, revised the text of the *Gold of Greece* catalogue and, with Angelos Delivorrias, edited the images reproduced in the present publication. Anna McFarland coordinated the myriad details associated with the exhibition's presentation in Dallas, and Emily Sano, Deputy Director of Collections and Exhibitions, effectively coordinated the national tour of *Gold of Greece.*

Thanks must be offered to the wonderfully supportive Governing Board of the Benaki Museum. The Trustees of the Dallas Museum of Art, so ably lead by Mr. Irvin L. Levy and Mr. C. Vincent Prothro, were also unstinting in their support of the project.

We are deeply grateful to our sponsor Corrigan's Jewelers and Executive Vice President, Mr. Nick White, for their willingness to fund this project and their vision in recognizing the extraordinary educational benefit that this exhibition will have in Texas. American Airlines and Olympic Airways are the official carriers of the exhibition and have generously provided transportation of personnel and works of art.

Richard R. Brettell
Director, Dallas Museum of Art

FOREWORD

Angelos Delivorrias
Director, Benaki Museum

The exhibition *Gold of Greece: Jewelry and Ornaments from the Benaki Museum*, sets out to highlight one of the fundamental factors that has shaped Greek culture, namely the uncommonly wide span of its history, reaching back into the mists of prehistoric time and marked by some of the most important achievements of the human mind and spirit: the mastery of language in all its wealth and diversity of expression, the impetus toward philosophical inquiry, the growth of historical self-awareness, the insights derived from social experimentation, the imaginative and sensitive approach to the natural environment and the creative urge to transform it by enhancing it. This continuity can be ascribed to two principal causes: the physical stamina of a people, always at a numerical disadvantage, in the face of a long chain of adverse historical circumstances, and the amazing resilence of the Greek language, which has succeeded in retaining the same vocabulary—and a corresponding poetic genius—from Homer to the major Greek poets of the 19th and 20th centuries. Another determining factor has been the versatility and adaptability of Greek intellectual and artistic aspirations in response to a constantly changing world. This serves to explain the many faces of Greek civilization as it evolved through its successive phases: Prehistoric, Archaic, Classical, Hellenistic, Roman, Byzantine, Neohellenic during the periods of Venetian and Ottoman rule, and finally Modern Greek.

The crucial thread running through this cultural continuity has always been the Greeks' embrace of the ideological principle of anthropocentrism. The optimism inherent in this outlook has produced a whole system of values that has continued to this day to shape human existence throughout the civilized world. This humanistic view of the universe must be counted as a lasting debt to the Hellenic spirit. Indeed, many aspects of Greek civilization remain among the most significant experiences of mankind. Time and again its teachings have proved firm points of reference, whether leading back to the very origins of intellectual and artistic creativity, or forward to the breakthroughs—or even the dead ends—of recent research. When put to the test, the value of Greek teachings has frequently been found to be strikingly relevant.

It would have been possible, of course, to mount an exhibition of items representing various aspects of artistic expression, whereby the essence of the Greek spirit might perhaps have been brought out more fully and made a more powerful impact. The selection, however, has been limited to gold jewelry, not only because the Benaki Museum's jewelry collection has the most comprehensive chronological coverage of all its Greek collections, but also because the use of gold and other metals reflects historical circumstances from the vitally important economic point of view, while at the same time mirroring the aesthetic predilections of each period.

If the Benaki exhibition succeeds in promoting a better understanding of the Greek cultural legacy, eliciting sensitive reactions on the part of the public and arousing a desire for personal involvement with Greek history and Greek lands, it will have fulfilled its aims. Then and only then will all those who were responsible for the planning and realization of this project feel that their work has not been in vain: the authors of this exhibition guidebook and a forthcoming catalogue, the staff of the Benaki Museum, the Dallas Museum of Art and the other museums where the exhibition is to be shown, the Greek Ministry of Culture under whose auspices the exhibition is presented, and the American sponsors who made its realization possible. The Administrative Board of the Benaki Museum feels deeply obliged to all these persons and organizations. Special debts of gratitude are owed to our valued friend Virginia Nick, who has done so much to bring this exhibition to fruition, and to Electra Georgoula, an invaluable colleague without whose tireless exertions and unfailingly resourceful expertise the present publication and the eagerly anticipated catalogue would never have seen the light of day. Finally, we should like to pay tribute to the ever-constructive collaboration of Dr. Richard Brettell, Director of the Dallas Museum of Art; it has been a truly rewarding experience to work with him.

Angelos Delivorrias
Director, Benaki Museum

INTRODUCTION

The Benaki Museum

The Benaki Museum differs from the other museums of Greece for three main reasons: first, because its collection of priceless artifacts offers an illuminating commentary on the entire span of Greek history from the Early Bronze Age to the inter-war period of the twentieth century; secondly, because of the unusually wide range and outstanding quality of its two self-contained collections, the Islamic Art department and the Chinese Ceramics department; and thirdly, because it was the first Greek museum to come into being through the far-sighted vision of a private collector, Anthony Benaki. The continuation of his life's work has been made possible not only by the Museum's independent status, which is a factor of vital importance, but also by the unfailing support of the State and the invaluable assistance received from private individuals. As a result the Museum has been able to establish a high reputation for itself and to win due recognition for its work, which owes much to its adaptability and its constant sensitivity to changing social conditions. The Benaki Museum is particularly fortunate in the exceptionally large number of important donations it receives from both named and anonymous benefactors, whether these consist of complete collections of works of art or historical documents, single masterpieces, or occasionally articles of a humbler kind, which are no less valuable in filling the gaps that inevitably exist in some of the collections.

The Benaki Museum was founded in April 1930 by Anthony Benaki (1873-1954), who came from an Alexandrian Greek family that played an active part in the political, social and cultural life of Greece. To obtain some idea of the atmosphere in which he grew up and acquired the beliefs and principles that governed his life, one has only to consider the many activities of his father. Emmanuel Benaki (1843-1929) was among the closest associates of Eleftherios Venizelos (1864-1936), one of the most eminent statesmen in Modern Greek history. The elder Benaki's name was linked with the founding of several public welfare institutions and he was known for his contribution to the rehabilitation of the refugees who poured into Greece after the 1922 Asia Minor disaster. Anthony's sister, Penelope Delta (1874-1941), was a prolific and talented writer

Anthony Benaki

whose work exerted a formative influence on the intellectual
standards of her time; her suicide was a tragic protest against the
German occupation of Greece in the Second World War. Anthony
Benaki was cast in the same mold. Not only was he totally commit-
ted to the work of founding the Museum, organizing it properly,
and constantly enriching its collections, a cause on which he spent
the whole of his personal fortune, but he also lent his support to
any undertaking which he believed would raise the cultural standards
of his country.

There can be no doubt that Anthony Benaki's character was also
shaped in its formative years by the moral and intellectual climate of
Alexandria, a climate which may be described as "cosmopolitan
Hellenocentrism" in the sense that it represented a well-balanced
blend of Western European intellectual attitudes, the traditions of
the Islamic East, and the aspirations of the large and prosperous
Greek community in Egypt. We must remember that Greece, as it
now stands, is the product of a long-running struggle to liberate
"unredeemed" areas of the mainland and islands and to bring them
within the frontiers of the independent Greek state—a struggle
that lasted from 1830 until the end of the Second World War—and
also that large sections of the Greek population were still scattered
outside those frontiers: in Constantinople, in the coastal cities and
hinterland of Asia Minor and the Pontus, and in numerous expatriate colonies elsewhere. The historical circumstances of the time,
which stemmed directly from the situation that had existed since
the 18th century, encouraged the trend towards emigration and
led to the establishment and growth of prosperous and highly
cultured communities in such far-flung places as Moscow and
Odessa, Bucharest, Budapest and Vienna, Trieste and Venice,
Alexandria and Cairo, Amsterdam, Paris and London, and many
cities in the United States.

Inevitably, these colonies of expatriate Greeks were haunted by
feelings of nostalgia for the ancient past and dreams of national
liberation and regeneration, feelings that were colored by the central
idea of historical continuity and also by the liberalism of progressive

movements in Europe, with which the Greeks of the diaspora were in close contact. Other unifying factors were the dynamic presence of the Orthodox Church and the astonishing resilience of the Greek language, both of which served as strong connecting links between the fragmented segments of the Greek world.

All this may help to explain how the tradition of benefaction towards the motherland came to be seen by Greeks of the diaspora as a national duty in the cause of Greece's rebirth. But even before then, during the War of Independence, expatriate Greek communities had borne much of the cost of arming the freedom fighters at home; and similarly, after the liberation, it was Greek émigrés who shouldered most of the expense of building educational establishments, cultural foundations and public welfare institutions, which the newly-independent Greek state badly needed in order to drag itself into the 19th century.

It is against this background that the foundation of the Benaki Museum should be viewed. The very special character of the Museum can only be understood in the context of that moral and intellectual climate that sought to unite the realities of the present, the call of the past, and the prospects for the future into a single dynamic whole, in which memories of what has been and visions of what is to come are vital ingredients of existence. The Museum building designed by Anastasios Metaxas, the architect who supervised the restoration of the marble Panathenaic Stadium for the first modern Olympic Games of 1896, is one of the finest examples of Athenian architecture in the late Neoclassical-Romantic style, and its imposing marble façade reflects the nostalgia for antiquity that was so characteristic of the rise of the urban middle class in post-liberation Greece.

All in all, the Benaki Museum of today may be compared to a large research center whose primary objective is to study the evolution of Hellenism over the ages and to present its findings to the widest possible public at home and abroad, seeking to include the layman as well as the scholar. There can be no doubt that the surest confirmation that a museum is successfully fulfilling its mission, lies in the public's response. In the case of the Benaki Museum this response takes the form of a deep-rooted conviction that the Museum can be relied upon to safeguard Greece's cultural heritage and to emphasize its continuity. This conviction is apparent not only in the heart-warming willingness of the Museum's many benefactors to donate some of their most precious heirlooms, not only in the regularity and frequency of daily visits and of attendance at the various special events organized by the Museum, but also in the atmosphere of public confidence and trust which strengthens the bonds of mutual goodwill and cooperation between the Museum and the community at large, and defines the framework of future obligations. And so, in accordance with the wishes of the founder, the successful performance of the Museum depends to a large extent on the dynamic participation of society as a whole.

Angelos Delivorrias

CHRONOLOGY

2800-1800 B.C.	Early Bronze Age
1800-1400 B.C.	Middle Bronze Age
1400-1200 B.C.	Late Bronze Age
	Late Helladic Period in Greece
c. 1200 B.C.	Fall of Troy
12th century B.C.	End of Mycenaean kingdoms
1000-700 B.C.	Geometric Period
700-650 B.C.	Orientalizing Period
	Age of Colonization
	Homer's *Iliad* (?)
650-480 B.C.	Archaic Period
490-479 B.C.	Wars with Persia
480-323 B.C.	Age of Classicism
	Dominance of Athens, 5th century
323 B.C.	Death of Alexander the Great
323 B.C.-31 B.C.	Hellenistic Age
146 B.C.	Roman conquest of Greece
31 B.C.	Battle of Actium
	Roman Empire rules Greek lands
313 A.D.	Roman Empire becomes Christian
324 A.D.	Constantinople becomes capital
395 A.D.	East and West Empires divide
527-565 A.D.	Justinian the Great, Emperor
726-787 A.D.	Iconoclastic controversy
867-1056 A.D.	Macedonian dynasty
1204 A.D.	Sack of Constantinople
1261-1453 A.D.	Paleologus dynasty
1453 A.D.	End of Byzantine Empire
1453-1830 A.D.	Turkish Domination of Greece
1830	Greece becomes an Independent State

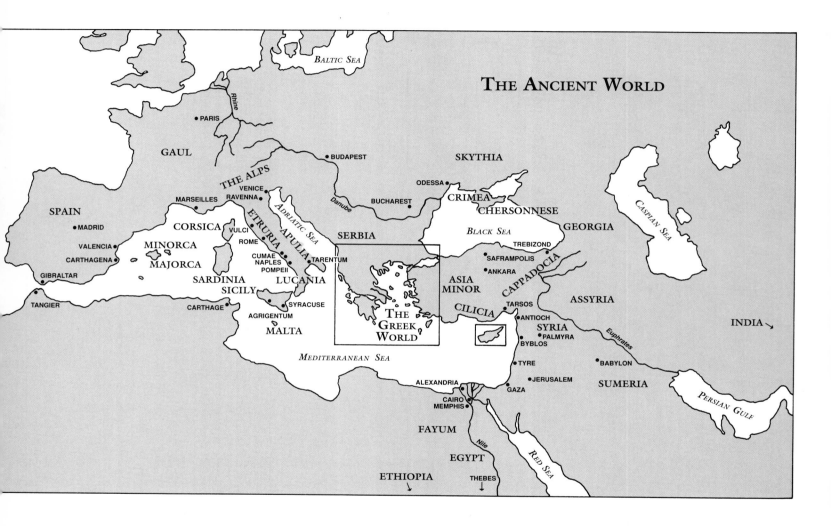

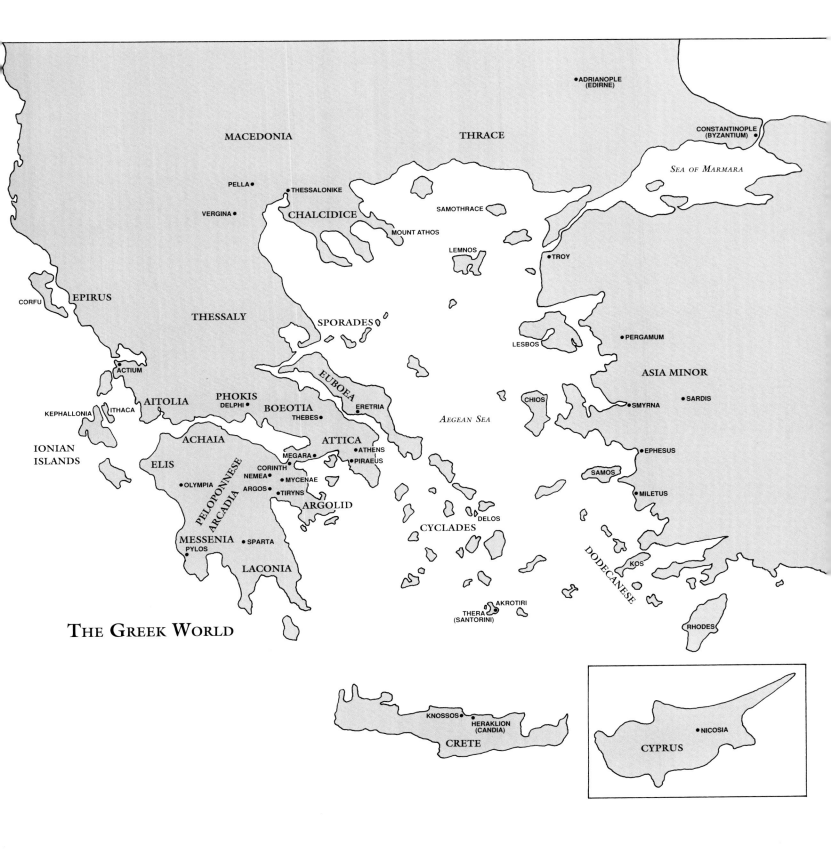

ADRIANOPLE
(EDIRNE)

CONSTANTINOPLE
(BYZANTIUM)

MACEDONIA

THRACE

SEA OF MARMARA

PELLA

THESSALONIKE

VERGINA

CHALCIDICE

SAMOTHRACE

MOUNT ATHOS

LEMNOS

TROY

CORFU

EPIRUS

THESSALY

SPORADES

PERGAMUM

LESBOS

ACTIUM

ASIA MINOR

AITOLIA

PHOKIS

BOEOTIA

EUBOEA

CHIOS

SMYRNA

SARDIS

KEPHALLONIA

ITHACA

DELPHI

THEBES

ERETRIA

Aegean Sea

IONIAN
ISLANDS

ACHAIA

ATTICA

ELIS

MEGARA

ATHENS

PIRAEUS

EPHESUS

OLYMPIA

CORINTH

NEMEA

MYCENAE

ARGOS

TIRYNS

SAMOS

MILETUS

PELOPONNESE

ARCADIA

ARGOLID

DELOS

CYCLADES

MESSENIA

SPARTA

PYLOS

DODECANESE

KOS

LACONIA

AKROTIRI

THERA
(SANTORINI)

RHODES

THE GREEK WORLD

KNOSSOS

HERAKLION
(CANDIA)

CRETE

NICOSIA

CYPRUS

SELECT GLOSSARY

Beading: Arranging single gold grains in lines or hammering wire into a groove cut with hemispherical depressions.

Bezel: The upper part of a finger ring, excluding the hoop and shoulders.

Cameo: Raised relief design, usually carved into a hardstone or gem.

Chasing: Working metal from the front, using a tool with a rounded end, so that the pattern is indented in the surface.

Enamel: Colored glass or vitreous glazes fused on a metal surface.

Enamelling:

CLOISONNE ENAMEL: A network of metal cloisons forming the outlines of a decorative design is soldered to a metal surface. This is filled with powdered enamel and fired.

PAINTED ENAMEL: A layer of wet powdered enamel is applied over the front and back of a thin copper sheet and fired. This supplies a base for scenes painted in colored enamels.

FILIGREE ENAMEL: A decorative pattern formed by twisted gold wire filled with enamel.

Engraving: Cutting patterns into a surface with a sharp tool.

Fibula: A brooch in safety pin form.

Filigree: A decorative pattern made of wires, either soldered to a background or left as openwork.

Gilding: The application of gold to the surface of an object made from another material.

Granulation: Soldering minute grains of gold to a background. In antiquity, the solder would have been invisible.

Intaglio: A sunk relief design in stone or metal; often used for seals, with the design in reverse.

Niello: A black compound of silver, lead, copper and sulphur applied to metal, in the manner of enamel.

Openwork: Any variety of open pattern, such as one formed by cutting out portions of metal with a chisel.

Opus Interrasile: Intricate pierced decoration made by cutting out a pattern in sheet gold using awls or chisels.

Pectoral: A form of ornament worn on the breast.

Protome: A projecting ornamental figurehead.

Repoussé: A technique of working sheet metal from behind with punches to raise the pattern, which stands in relief on the front. Also called embossing.

Soldering: Joining two metal surface with a fused metal alloy.

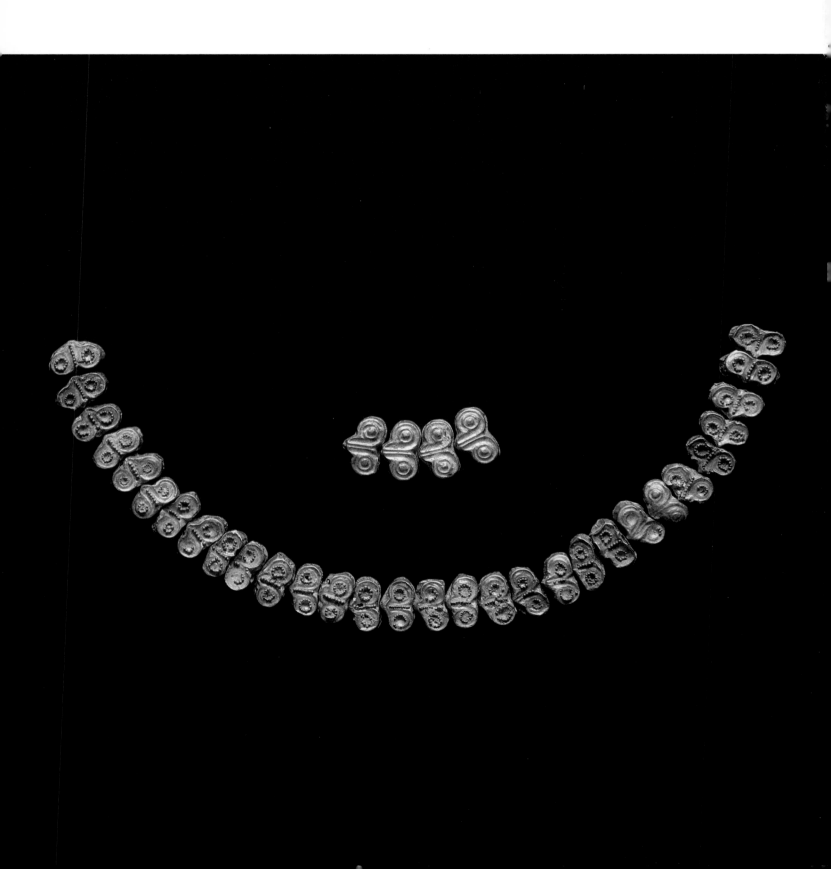

In the last half of the second millennium B.C., the mainland of Greece was dominated by wealthy and powerful rulers, whose kingdoms centered upon fortified palaces, such as the great hill of Mycenae in the Peloponnese, from which the Mycenaean Period takes its name. These early Greek-speaking peoples were warriors, traders and free-booters, who had extensive contacts all over the eastern Mediterranean world. Their art reveals close ties with work from Egypt, the Levant and Minoan Crete. The extraordinary wealth of goldwork and jewelry found in the royal graves at Mycenae indicates both great economic prosperity and a profound belief in the symbolic importance of display for a ruler's self-glorification, both in this life and in the afterworld (*fig. 1*). Homer's epic description of Mycenae as a city "rich in gold" has been completely borne out by archaeological excavation.

The Mycenaean Greeks probably learned advanced techniques of metalworking, such as granulation, filigree and cloisonné, from Crete, which in turn had derived its own jewelry tradition from Egypt and the Middle East by way of Syria, as far back as the third millennium B.C. Much Mycenaean ornament is an amalgam of the naturalistic and free-flowing Minoan Cretan style with the Mycenaean taste for symmetrical heraldic compositions. By the late 15th century, some Mycenaeans seem already to have settled in Crete, absorbing the older Minoan civilization. In turn, Cretan craftsmen probably were working at Mycenaean sites on the mainland. For the next two hundred years, an hybrid style of jewelry, using sophisticated techniques of manufacture, was common in the Mycenaean world. Much of this jewelry and fine metalwork was buried with dead rulers in monumental tombs, to signify the splendors of their reign. The late Mycenaean *koine*, or common style, produced very lavish ornaments, though mass production sometimes led to a decline in fresh artistic inspiration. Objects like rings or seal stones (*fig. 2*) were used to indicate rank

FIG. 1
Lily-shaped necklace beads
MYCENAEAN PERIOD

FIG. 2
Lentoid seal
MYCENAEAN PERIOD

and social power, in addition to the more feminine use of jewelry as an adornment of sexual allure. Motifs used in late Mycenaean jewelry are often derived from an earlier Minoan repertory, including papyrus flowers, lilies, seashells, octopuses, Minoan *daemons*, libation vessels, figure-of-eight shields and altars.

The impression left by early Greek jewelry is that of a wealthy and sophisticated society, with many connections outside Greece itself, some as far away as the Baltic Sea. The production of this jewelry was controlled by palace workshops, whose managers would have been able to deal with the importation of rare materials (*fig. 3*), the supervision of skilled craftsmen and the purchase of foreign objects,

FIG. 3
Necklace of semi-precious stones
MYCENAEAN PERIOD

FIG. 4
Ring with plain bezel
MYCENAEAN PERIOD

such as the collection of oriental cylinder seals found at the palace workshop in Thebes. Palace records at Pylos refer to precious materials like *kuruso* (gold), *akuro* (silver), *kuwano* (lapis lazuli or blue glass paste), *erepa* (ivory), and *paraku* (emerald). Records at Mycenae refer to *kuwano-woko* (goldsmiths) (*fig. 4*). These workshops presumably supplied ornaments for trade, as well as for the needs of the local court.

Drawing on painted frescoes and figurines, as well as Homer's epic poems, which refer back to the Mycenaean Age from a later period, it is possible to define the use of jewelry in these early Greek kingdoms. Women used gold ornaments to hold their elaborate hairdos in place and to pin together their garments. They also wore diadems, earrings, necklaces, rings, bracelets and anklets. Gold foil and beads were often sewn onto fine garments. Men wore similar kinds of jewelry to indicate their high rank at the top of a rigidly hierarchic society. Diadems, amulets, necklaces and signet rings (*fig. 5*) were used for the display of power and were finally buried with the ruler in his tomb. Offerings of precious ornaments were also devoted to the honored dead.

FIG. 5
Ring with cloisonné bezel
MYCENAEAN PERIOD

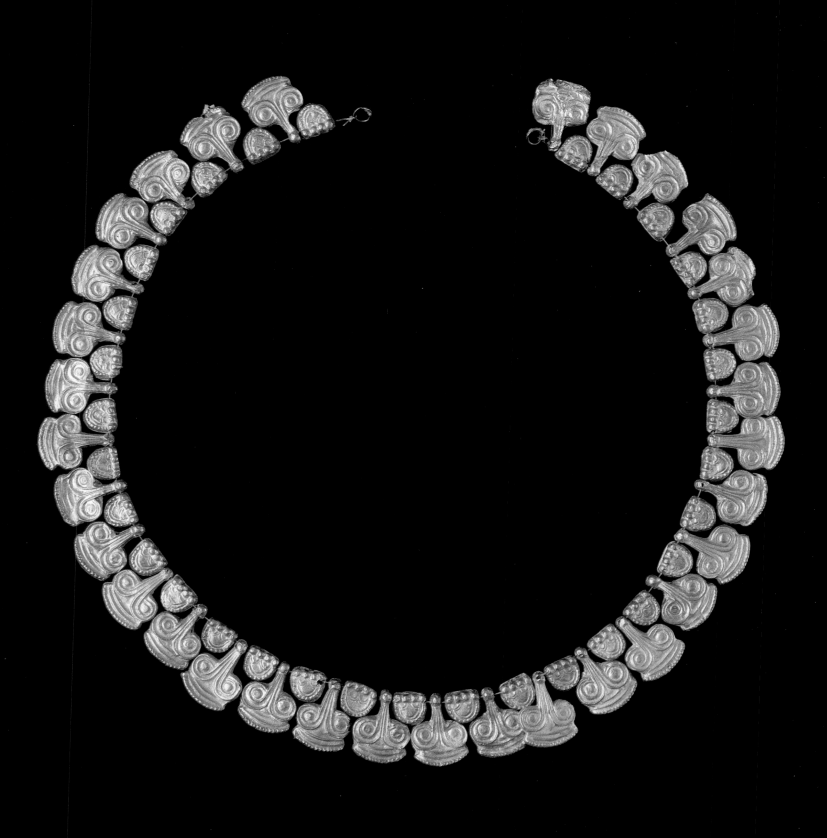

PLATE 1
*Necklace with
lily-shaped beads*
MYCENAEAN PERIOD
(opposite)

The hybrid plants represented
in this elaborate necklace of
repoussé beads derive from the
Egyptian papyrus flower, sacred
to the snake goddess of the
Egyptian delta, and from the
Minoan sacred lily flower.
Such stylized ornamental plant
forms were popular in different
media, as may be seen in the
majestic "Prince of the Lilies"
fresco from the palace at
Knossos in Crete, on which the
prince wears a papyrus-lily
necklace, or on frescoes from
Akrotiri, where the rigging of
ships is hung with similar
necklaces.

PLATE 2
Pendants
MYCENAEAN PERIOD

These two pendants, which
would have been attached to
necklaces, were made by
molding gold foil over a core
or matrix in the desired shape.
Both figures were probably
amulets, with a symbolic or
sacral meaning. The figure-of-
eight shield, a common means
of military defense in the late
Bronze Age, also appears
frequently in ritual scenes as an
attribute of a goddess. Jewelry
like the Benaki piece may have
belonged to a priest. The lion
was an even more widespread
sacred figure in the ancient
Near East, as kings and rulers
were believed to assume a
lion's ferocious power.

PLATE 3
Rosette appliqués
Mycenaean Period

Each of the five elegant rosettes
was made by lightly tapping
gold foil over a matrix and then
cutting around the petal
shapes. Such ornaments were
sewn on cloth or leather
garments. Many of these
repoussé foil ornaments have
been found in wealthy
Mycenaean burials, where they
adorned either the actual
clothes of the dead or their
winding sheets. From pictures
of Mycenaean garments in
fresco paintings, it seems likely
that these rosettes ornamented
a belt.

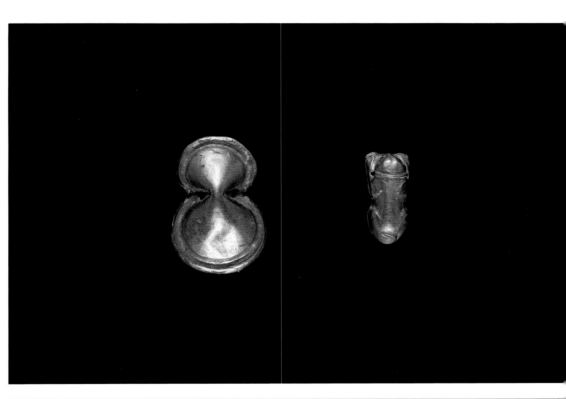

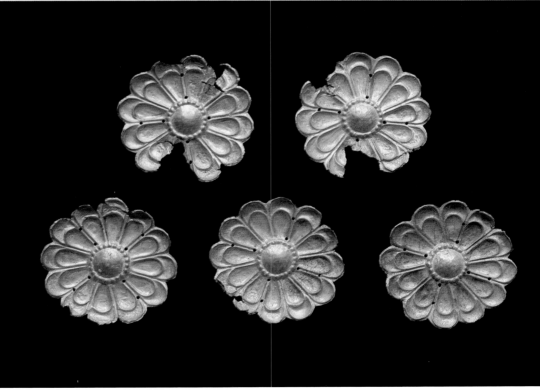

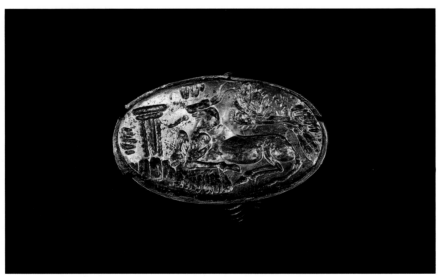

PLATES 4, 5, 6
Signet ring, signet ring, cylinder seal
MYCENAEAN PERIOD

Signet rings, generally made of gold, are among the most characteristic of all Creto-Mycenaean jewelry and display the highest standard of Aegean workmanship. The appearance of such rings in elite Mycenaean graves from the 16th through the l2th centuries B.C. indicates that they were a symbol of power. Plate 4 features a solid gold ring with a scene showing a goddess and a young man in a shrine setting, probably indicative of the Cretan sacred marriage. Plate 5, which depicts a sacrificial bull, is a good example of Cretan naturalism in art. While the Near Eastern sealstone was less common than signet rings in the Aegean area, local imitations, like Plate 6 with its scene of female celebrants, do occur.

PLATE 7
*Pair of earrings in form
of bull heads*
MYCENAEAN PERIOD

These two identical gold
earrings in the form of bull
heads were made of sheet
gold stamped in relief and
ornamented with gold wire.
Such handsomely stylized
earrings are typical of
Mycenaean sites in Cyprus.
Although the bull was a
sacred animal on Crete,
earrings of this sort are more
common in the Mycenaean
settlements on Cyprus than
in the Aegean area itself.

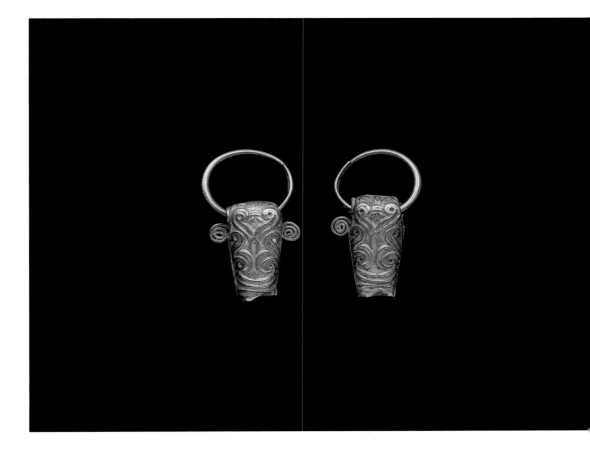

From Geometric To Archaic Greece

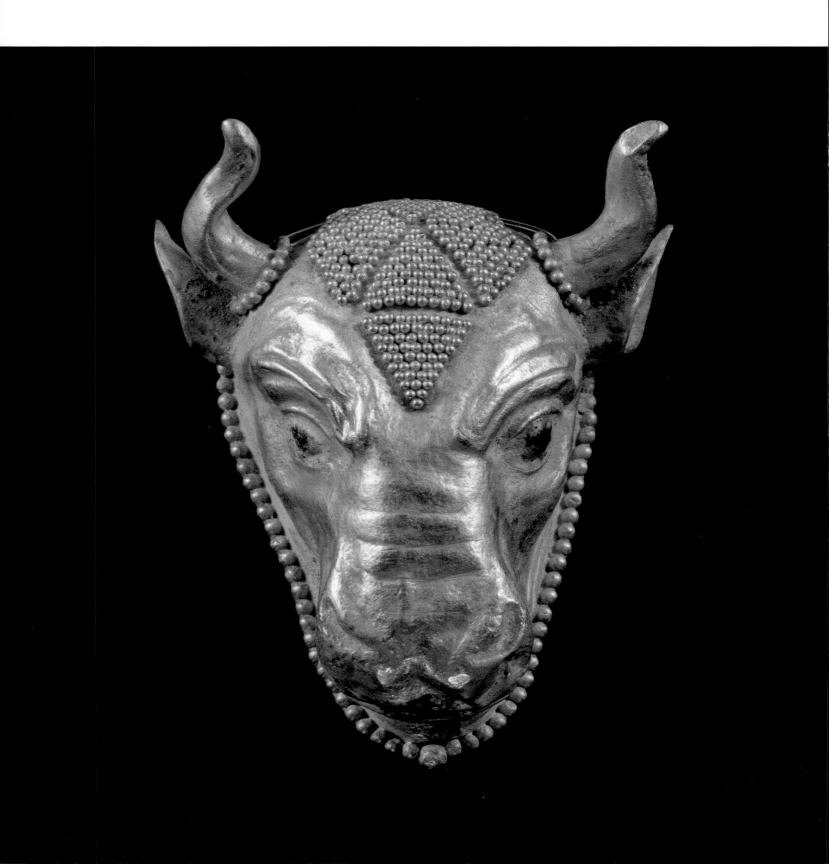

FIG. 8
Pin
GEOMETRIC PERIOD

The long span of time from the end of the Mycenaean Age to the Archaic Period witnessed an initial decline followed by a great outburst of creativity in Greek art (*fig. 6*). By the twelfth century B.C., the Mycenaean kingdoms were in a state of collapse. The whole of the eastern Mediterranean was undergoing a period of turmoil and invasion at this time, but mainland Greece reverted to a less civilized way of life, without the use of writing, monumental architecture and extensive trade contacts abroad, which had marked Mycenaean societies. It was during this Dark Age from the eleventh to the ninth centuries, however, that the foundations of classical Greek culture were laid. Geometric style art, in particular, had a logical clarity of form based on an intellectual grasp of the essential character of objects, which was to be significant in later Greek art.

There is little jewelry surviving from these post-Mycenaean centuries, but an important shift in technology occurred, with the replacement of bronze by iron for tools and weapons. Since less gold was available than in the Mycenaean period, bronze came to be used for ornaments like pins, necklaces or the fibulas that fastened parts of garments together (*fig. 7, fig. 8*). Like the vase painters, from whose ceramics the Geometric period was named, metalworkers began to introduce figural motifs into their ornamental designs by the ninth century B.C.

FIG. 6
Bull's head pendant
ARCHAIC PERIOD
(opposite)

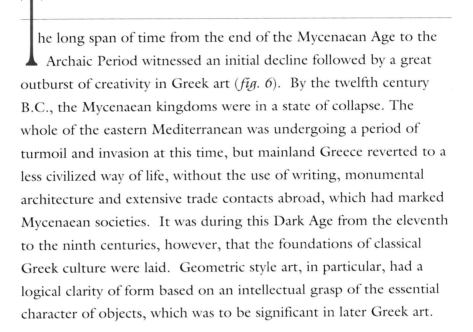

FIG. 7
Group of five amulets
GEOMETRIC PERIOD

By the eighth century, Greek horizons had again widened. Greek colonies were established from the Black Sea to the Western Mediterranean and trade was resumed with the Near East. Through the influence of the Phoenician alphabet, writing again was used in the Greek states. Stimulated by the rich repertory of Near Eastern craftsmanship, Greek art, including jewelry, adopted motifs like plant and animal forms, or mythic beings like sphinxes (*see cover & plate 12*), griffins and winged horses. By the seventh century, the human form and mythological scenes began to appear. The gold jewelry of this Orientalizing period reached a very high level of taste and manufacture.

Orientalizing jewelry is well-known, because great pieces with superb filigree ornament were dedicated as offerings in major Greek sanctuaries at Delphi, Olympia and Samos. This work reflects a balance between fantastic Near Eastern motifs and a sober Greek interest in the natural world. Gold was once again available as a raw material and skilled craftsmen must have existed at all the major Greek centers.

The Age of Colonization led to a brilliant period for the Greek city-states, based on commerce and trade. The Archaic Greek societies of the sixth century B.C. used jewelry as both a symbol of

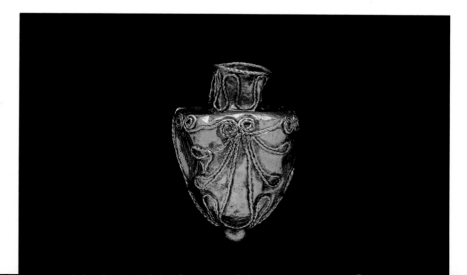

Fig. 9
Vase-shaped pendant
Archaic Period

FIG. 10
Necklace
ARCHAIC PERIOD

economic success and as a valuable trade good (*fig. 9*). This same period saw the first great experiments in philosophy and science, so it is not surprising that sixth century art also emphasized individual personality and intellectual freedom. Leaders of city-states, like Polykrates on Samos or the Peisistratid family of tyrants in Athens, were known to revel in the display of costly personal ornaments.

Jewelry favored by the elite of Archaic Greek society shared the experimental humanism of contemporary painting and sculpture. Such aesthetic ideals as the transcendent beauty of a nude male figure or the grace and modesty of the draped female form occur in jewelry, though on a smaller scale (*see plate 13*). The mastery of narrative flow achieved by relief sculpture affected composition in gold ornament, too. Despite the comparatively small amount of Archaic ornament that has survived, extant examples indicate that craftsmen continued to work in Orientalizing styles, but with a greater degree of naturalism. It is at this time that enamel began to be used for color effects. On the eve of the Persian Wars in the early fifth century B.C., Archaic Greece could command a sophisticated repertory of work in precious metals (*fig. 10*).

The origin of the spectacle fibula goes back to Central Europe during the Urnfield Period (13th to 11th centuries B.C.). In Greece, these elaborate bronze dress fasteners, which were worn in pairs on each shoulder to hold together large pieces of fabric, were common from the 11th century B.C. on. The double spiral shape, resembling a modern pair of eyeglasses, was made from a single piece of bronze wire.

The island of Rhodes was a major production center for jewelry in the Orientalizing Period. It was also a source for Near Eastern motifs, which passed from Rhodes to the West by way of ceramics, fabrics and metalwork of all kinds. This fragmentary diadem is a good example of Rhodian style, which often combined repoussé, granulation and filigree. The motifs of sphinxes, rosettes, heads in Daedalic style, and bull heads are typical of Orientalizing ornament. Although the diadem was ultimately placed in a tomb, it was probably worn in life on festive occasions.

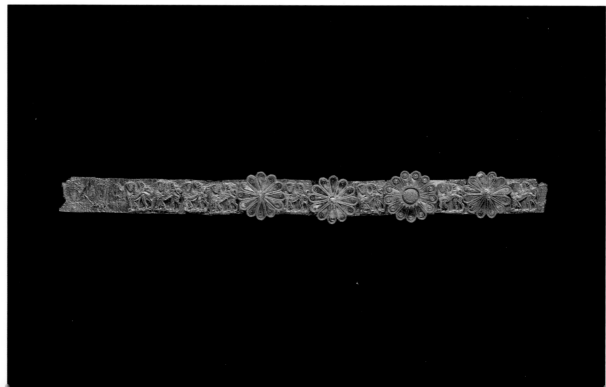

PLATE 10
Gorgoneion
Archaic Period

The monstrous demon face of
the gorgoneion, or Medusa
head, was one of the most
common subjects in antiquity.
Just as Medusa's face could
turn men to stone, the gorgon
image was believed to avert
evil. Hence, it appears on the
goddess Athena's *aegis* and
on soldiers breastplates, also.
This gold foil ornament was
made to be attached as a
protective amulet on a dead
person's clothes.

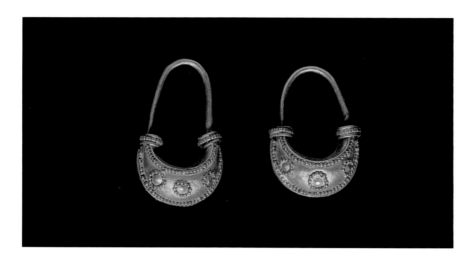

Plate 11
Boat earrings
ARCHAIC PERIOD

The boat earring was of Eastern origin, stemming from Sumerian prototypes. It remained popular in Greece from the Bronze Age to the Hellenistic period. The Benaki example, with primitive granulation, dates to the late 6th century B.C.

Plate 12
Pair of sphinxes
ARCHAIC PERIOD

Sphinxes, imaginary creatures that were part lion, part woman and part bird, were among the most popular of the fantastic Near Eastern animals which entered the Greek repertory in the 7th century B.C. In meaning, sphinxes range from symbols of wisdom, as in the story of Oedipus, to death demons placed in tombs. These fine late Archaic sphinxes perhaps decorated an elaborate utensil or a small piece of furniture. Despite the miniature scale, they are masterpieces of elegantly stylized decoration.

PLATE 13
Ring with kneeling archer
ARCHAIC PERIOD

Intaglio rings were very popular in antiquity, both to seal documents or property, and to identify a private individual. They are common in graves, but are also found as offerings in sanctuaries. The intaglio on this gold ring features a scene of a kneeling archer testing his bow, a popular device for circular compositions, such as jewelry, coins, or the central medallions of painted ceramic cups. The treatment of the archer's muscular body has parallels in both vase painting and sculpture of the late Archaic period.

THE CLASSICAL AGE

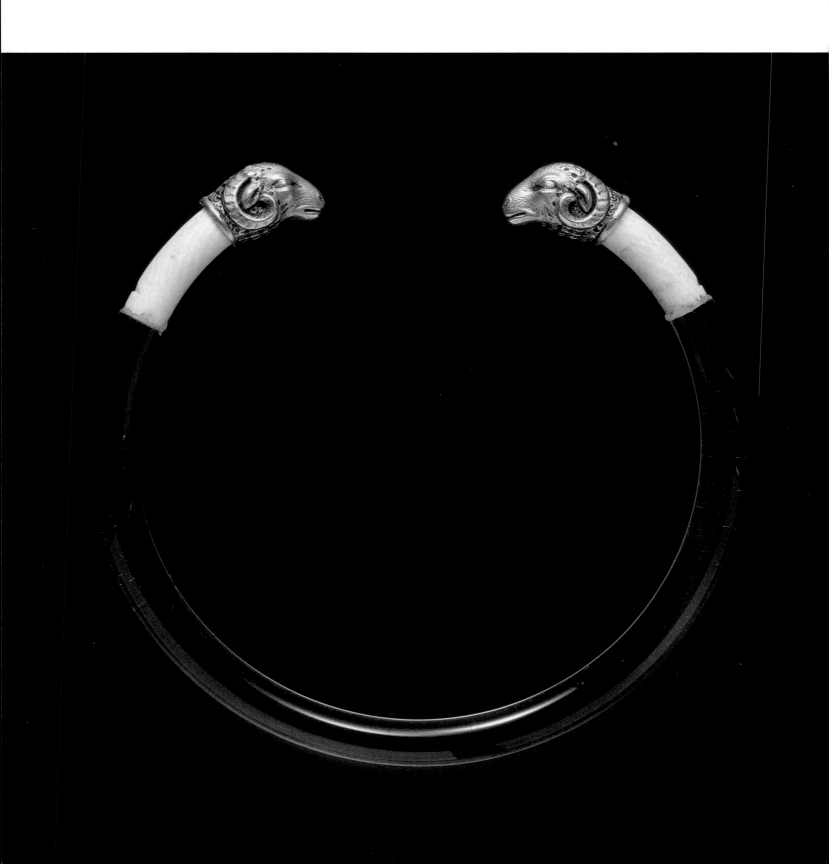

he success of Athens and her allied Greek city-states in repelling invasion by the Persian Empire in the decade 490-479 B.C. led to the Golden Age of Classical Greece. Through most of the fifth century, Athens was the dominant Greek city, and it is Athenian art which has set the standard of Greek classicism, but the other Greek states, including the wealthy city of Syracuse in Sicily, also enjoyed a period of prosperity and creativity.

Commerce continued to be essential to Greek life. Athens, the city of the Goddess of Wisdom, was a major economic center in the Mediterranean, as well as the fountainhead of philosophy and political democracy. Under her great leader Perikles, Athens was determined to retain control of the seas for political and commercial reasons, which led to numerous conflicts with her allies. In this vibrant competitive world, precious jewelry played a strong role (*fig. 11*).

The style of classical art was the finest expression of Greek interest in idealization, self-knowledge, and the humanist study of man in relation to his environment. The Good, the True and the Beautiful of philosophic thought were embodied in radiant human form. Though jewelry, an inherently decorative medium, continued the

FIG. 11
Bracelet with rams heads
(fragmentary)
CLASSICAL PERIOD
(opposite)

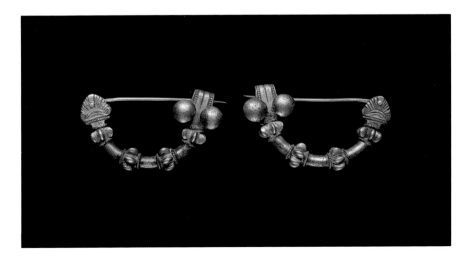

FIG. 12
Pair of bow fibulae
CLASSICAL PERIOD

Fig. 13
Two bow fibulae
Classical Period

models of the Archaic Period well into the fifth century, shape and form assumed the expressive grandeur of classic art (*fig. 12, fig. 13*). Colored enamels were now widely used to complement the pure glow of gold. Intricately wrought appliqué elements from the plant and animal world, like bees and flowers, decorate nobly simplified jewelry forms. In miniature, these earrings, necklaces and pendants express the figural idealism of classic art, found at its greatest in the Parthenon sculptures by Pheidias, or the single sculptural figures of Polykleitos.

The different types of jewelry developed in the fifth century continued to be elaborated in the fourth century, after the Peloponnesian War brought an end to the Athenian Empire. Fourth century figures in relief or figurative ornaments are truly parallel to works of monumental sculpture (*fig. 14*). Despite inter-city warfare, the fourth century was a period of considerable prosperity in the Greek states and one of increasing splendor and power for the royal court of Macedonia. Standards of craftsmanship in repoussé, chasing, casting, filigree and inlaid enamel were very high (*fig. 15*). The finds of royal Macedonian jewelry from the Vergina tombs has revealed this mastery of the art of goldsmith work in great detail.

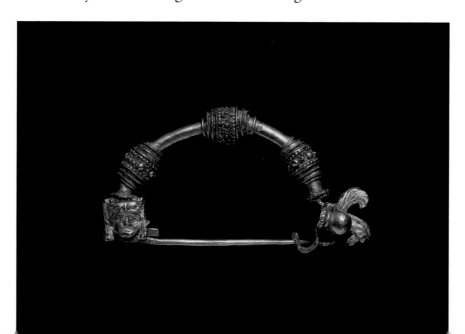

Fig. 14
Bow fibula
Classical Period

FIG. 15
Necklace of gold beads
CLASSICAL PERIOD

PLATE 14
Pair of snake head bracelets
CLASSICAL PERIOD

These bracelets are made of heavy sheet silver and are hollow inside. Judging by the size of the bracelets, as well as their resemblance to other examples, this pair belonged to a little girl and were buried with her. Snakes were popular motifs in jewelry, because they were considered protective spirits for the household.

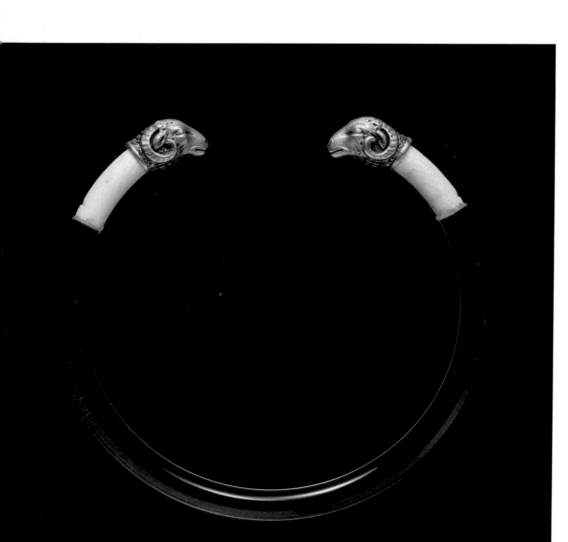

PLATE 15
Bracelet with rams heads
(fragmentary)
CLASSICAL PERIOD

The type of ram-headed bracelet, with the head made separately and sleeved over the bracelet hoop, had a tradition in Greek jewelry going back to the 8th century B.C. A revival of the type in the Classical Period was influenced in part by the splendid examples of Achaemenid Persian jewelry. These ram's heads are treated in a luxuriant naturalistic style dating to the late 5th or early 4th centuries B.C.

PLATE 16
*Earring with
pyramidal pendant*
CLASSICAL PERIOD

Earrings with cone-shaped
pendants decorated with gold
globules were widely popular
in Archaic and Classical Greek
jewelry. This example, with
its snake-like suspension loop,
is virtually sculptural in its
densely modelled form.

PLATE 17
*Earring with
vase-shaped pendant*
CLASSICAL PERIOD

Although vase-shaped pendants
suspended on wire appear
on coins of 479 B.C., actual
examples like the Benaki piece,
which dates to the early 4th
century B.C., are quite rare.
Similar pendants used as ear
drops are found further west,
where they appear as a feature
of Etruscan jewelry.

PLATE 18
Pair of bow fibulae
CLASSICAL PERIOD

These beaded fibulae with
protomes of the winged horse
Pegasus belong to an elaborate
variation of a Northern Greek
type. The Pegasus motif
entered Greek art during the
Orientalizing phase of the 7th
century B.C., and became
popular again in the 4th
century B.C. The motif had a
natural appeal to a society of
horse-owners, but the story of
Pegasus and the Greek hero,
Bellerophon, also expressed a
powerful Hellenic ideal, that of
Man taming brute Nature.

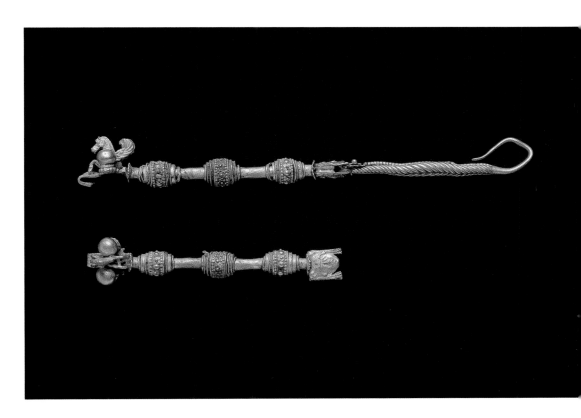

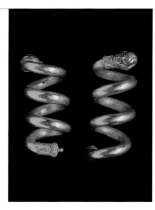

PLATE 19
Pair of spiral ornaments
CLASSICAL PERIOD

Each of these gold-covered bronze spiral ornaments terminate at one end in a rosette and at the other in a woman's head. Such ornaments are usually found in pairs, placed in a woman's grave near the body. While versions of these ornaments seen on Archaic statuettes seem to have been used as hair grips or earrings, these may have been dress fasteners.

PLATE 20
Vase pendant
CLASSICAL PERIOD

Originally, this fancifully ornamented vase pendant had two handles, by which it would have been suspended from a chain or earring. The body of the vase is made of two hemispheres of gold foil soldered together and covered with granulated decoration in a zig-zag pattern. Similar pieces date to the later 4th century B.C.

(bottom view of Plate 21)

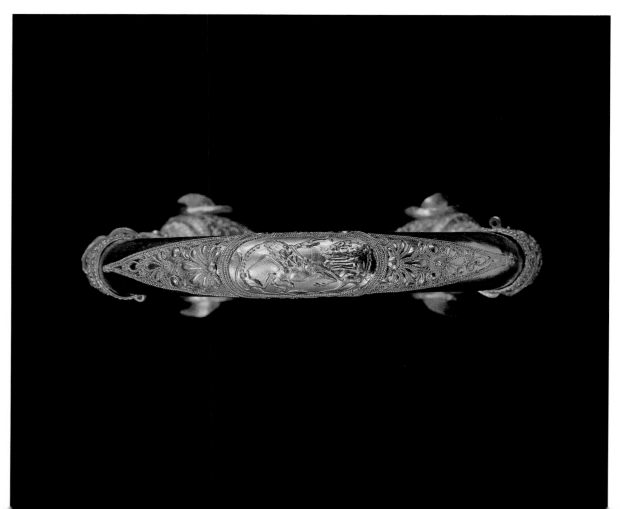

PLATE 21
Bracelet with rams heads
CLASSICAL PERIOD

Following the introduction of animal-headed bracelets from the Near East in the 7th century B.C., Greek versions of this style became increasingly elaborate. The hoop was embellished with filigree and granulation, forming a transition from the modelled head to the smooth surface of the metal. In this example, which has parallels in 4th-century B.C. Greek work from South Russia, there are several zones of ornamental decoration below the rams heads. Representations of rams were used to protect the wearer from disease and as symbols of potency.

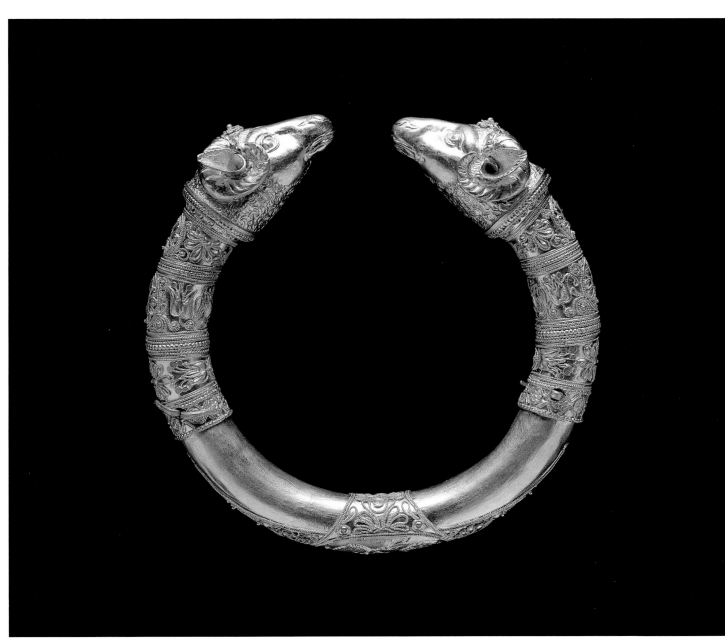

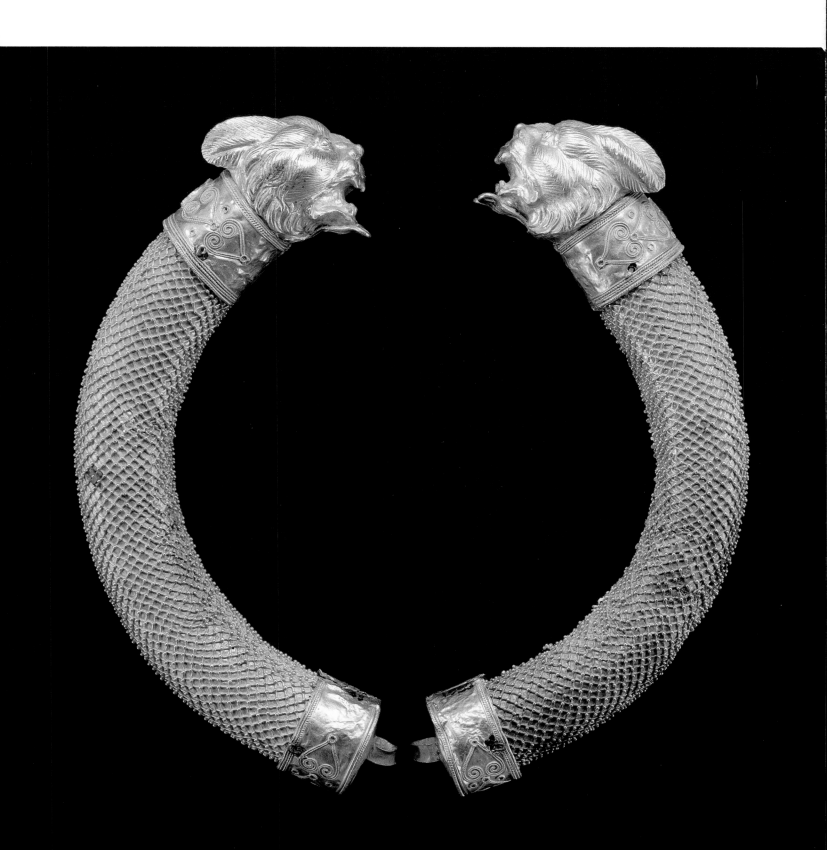

In the late fourth century B.C., Alexander the Great, inheriting the kingdom of Macedonia from his father Phillip, conquered the Near East and travelled as far as India. In a few dazzling years Greek civilization was transplanted to Asia Minor, Syria, Egypt and Persia. The Hellenistic Age, which Alexander inaugurated and his successors continued, was an international society with a Greek-speaking upper class. As the Greek cities in the western Mediterranean remained powerful also, Greek culture dominated a single economic zone from Spain to the borders of India. Greek merchants traded with Carthage, Ethiopia, India, China, Scythia and the hinterlands of the Balkans. This enlargement of the frontiers of Greece resulted not only in the diffusion of Greek language and culture, but in the unification of their basic characteristics. Art became a medium of cultural exchange (*fig. 16*).

Hellenistic art emphasized extremes of feeling, rather than classic restraint. Nostalgic sentiment alternated with a tough realism, while the strongly emotional and expressive style known as Hellenistic Baroque dealt freely with anguish and pathos. This more worldly approach to style affected jewelry also. Early Greek models were extensively reproduced for a consumer culture (*fig. 17*), while an

FIG. 16
Torque with lynx-head finials
HELLENISTIC PERIOD
(opposite)

FIG. 17
Pair of earrings with bull heads
HELLENISTIC PERIOD

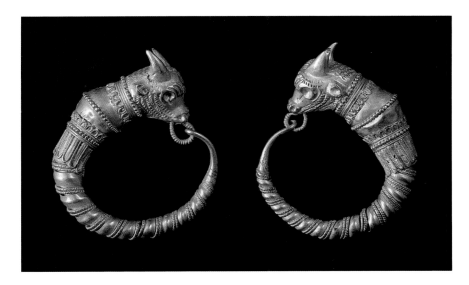

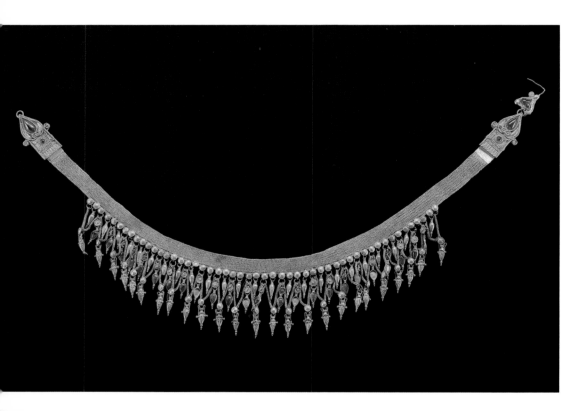

Fig. 18
Necklace with rows of pendants
Hellenistic Period

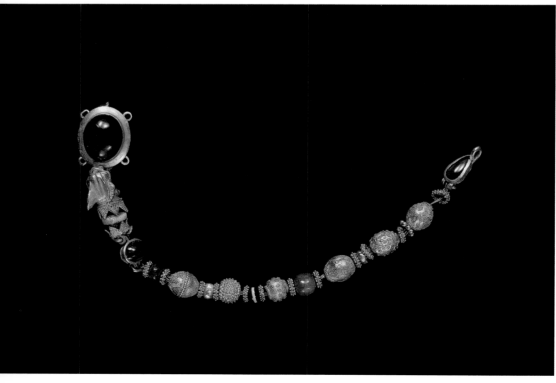

Fig. 19
Part of necklace
Hellenistic Period

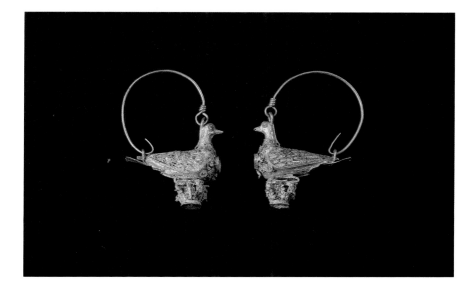

FIG. 20
*Pair of earrings
with doves*
HELLENISTIC PERIOD

international approach to craftsmanship assimilated exotic foreign styles with which the Greeks came in contact. Such cosmopolitan jewelry aimed at the maximum of luxurious display (*fig. 18*).

There was an ever-growing interest in polychromy, as indicated by extensive use of gemstones like garnet, carnelian, beryl, amethyst, emerald and rock crystal (*fig. 19*). Poorer work might imitate these effects with colored glass paste. The great increase in the use of gold indicates how the Greeks were now exploiting gold sources in conquered territories. Thematically, jewelry continued to use traditional motifs derived from the plant and animal world (*fig. 20*) or from mythology. Aphrodite and small *erotes*, the divinities of love, were especially appropriate for women's jewelry (*fig. 21*).

FIG. 21
*Pair of earrings
with erotes*
EARLY HELLENISTIC PERIOD

PLATE 22
*Pair of earrings with
vase-shaped pendants*
HELLENISTIC PERIOD
(opposite)

From the late 4th century
B.C. on, vase-shaped pendants
were much in vogue as
earrings and had a wide
geographical distribution in
the Mediterranean world.
The sober grandeur of this
Benaki pair, with a restrained
use of green glass gem stones
and simplified filigree on the
body of the vase, marks an
early, more sculptural, phase
of this type of jewelry.

PLATE 23
Bracelet with rams heads
HELLENISTIC PERIOD

The classical tradition of
rams-headed bracelets
continued into the early
Hellenistic period. Such
works were considered as
amulets to protect the wearer
from illness and to increase
a man's potency. In this
example, the relief work
around the muzzle and eye
of the ram finials is particularly
fine and lifelike.

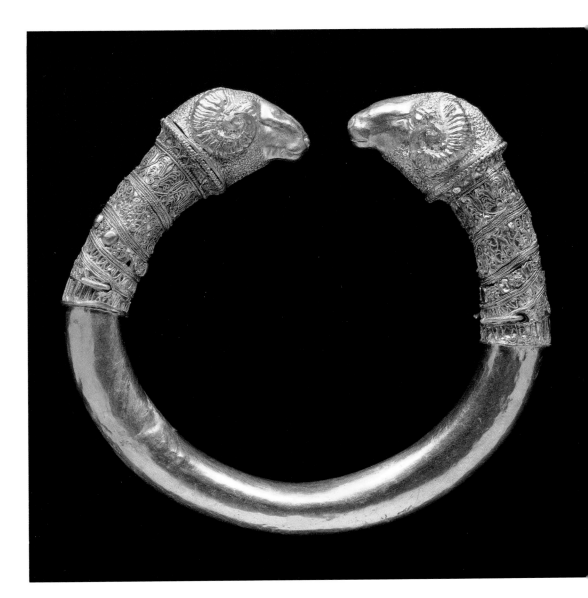

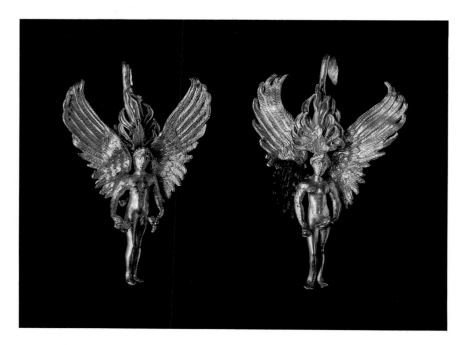

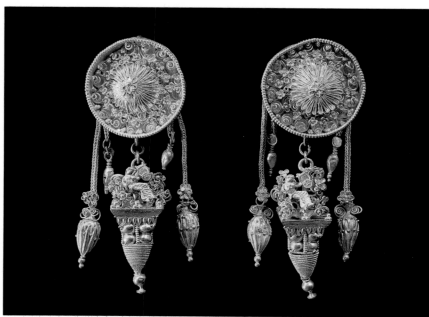

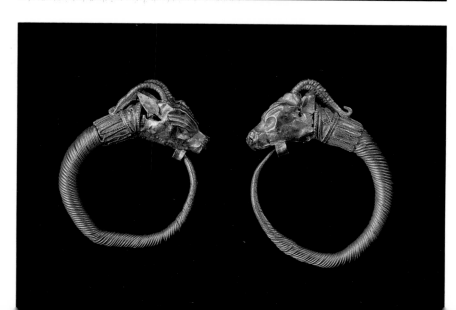

PLATE 24
*Pair of earrings
with erotes*
HELLENISTIC PERIOD

Each of this pair of earrings
consists of a naked Eros
(the child deity of love) with
outstretched wings. The
youthful figures hold an
offertory *phiale*, the sign of a
god, in one hand, while in the
other they hold a curved piece
of beaded wire representing a
rabbit-hunting stick. One
reason for the popularity of
rabbit-hunting motifs in
women's jewelry is the fact
that rabbits were favorite gifts
between lovers. While love
deities were also especially
suitable for female jewelry,
flying figures had a wider
connotation to the Greeks of
the pursuit of happiness.

PLATE 25
*Pair of earrings
with lyre-player*
HELLENISTIC PERIOD

An earring design with figures
placed between the ornamental
disc and the pendant goes back
to the early classical period.
Here, the lavish figure of
a woman playing a lyre,
presumably one of the muses,
might suggest happiness in
the Elysian Fields of the
Afterworld, since the jewelry
was probably placed in a
grave, or, more generally, the
ennobling character of music,
which was a central Greek art
form. The crowded naturalistic
style of the figures, framed
in luxuriant tendrils and
ornament, represents a high
point in elaborate Greek
goldsmith work.

PLATE 26
*Pair of earrings
with antelope heads*
HELLENISTIC PERIOD

Antelopes were quite
popular as a motif in early
Hellenistic art, since they
were believed to pull the
chariot of Eros, and therefore
had similar romantic and
erotic associations. The female
wearer of such jewelry could
be compared metaphorically
to the grace, charm and swift
motion of the antelope. The
heads of the antelopes are
embossed, with chased details,
while the ears and horns were
forged and soldered separately.

PLATE 27
*Pair of earrings with
lion griffin protomes*
HELLENISTIC PERIOD

The complex figurative work
on the griffin-head protomes
of these earrings includes
embossing, engraving, and
the use of blue glass paste for
the eyes. The lion griffin
type of earring originated
in 9th-century B.C. Assyria,
but spread far and wide in
the Mediterranean world.
By Hellenistic times, Greek
lion griffins had lost their
connections with Near Eastern
mythology and were associated
with Dionysos, the god of
wine and fertility, whose erotic
powers were often symbolized
by attendant lions and
panthers.

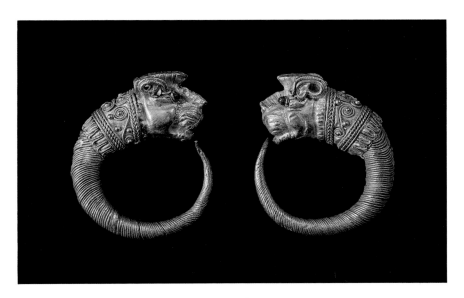

PLATE 28
*Pin with a figure
of Aphrodite*
HELLENISTIC PERIOD

Straight pins were used to
fasten clothes in Greece from
the 3rd millennium B.C. on.
Pin heads offered many
ornamental possibilities,
ranging from simple lobes
and spirals to figures of birds,
animals and flowers. Pins were
also dedicated as offerings in
temples. In this very complex
example, a Corinthian style
column forms the base for a
miniature sculptural group,
which consists of Aphrodite,
the goddess of love, drying
her hair, surrounded by *erotes*.
The pose of Aphrodite is
modelled on a famous statue
of a kneeling Aphrodite
wringing out her hair, and is
as impressive on this miniature
scale as it is in monumental
marble sculpture.

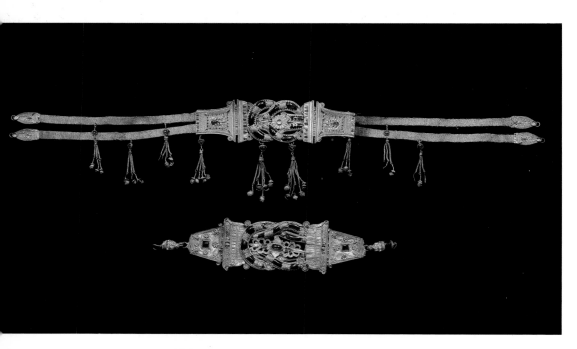

PLATE 29
Diadems
HELLENISTIC PERIOD

The two diadems were among a group of objects and coins supposed to have been found in a single treasure horde in Thessaly. Representing some of the finest work to be seen in the Benaki collections, this jewelry is dateable to the 2nd century B.C. Both of these diadems are made of braided straps with a central Knot of Herakles and include colored stone ornaments. According to the Roman writer Pliny, the decorative device of the Knot of Herakles could cure wounds, and its popularity in Hellenistic jewelry does suggests that it was thought to have apotropaic power.

PLATE 30
Medallion with bust of Athena
HELLENISTIC PERIOD

In this image of Athena, the warrior goddess of wisdom and patron of the city of Athens is shown wearing a triple-crested helmet, with her head fully modelled in the round and with eyes that were once inlaid with colored enamel or glass. The bust is rendered in bold relief from a single sheet of gold. A similar level of high craftsmanship may be seen in the exceptionally detailed moldings that frame the image. While the use of such medallions is unknown, the most likely theory is that they served as ornamental hair nets, attached by chains to a woman's bun of hair.

PLATE 31
Loutrophoros earring
HELLENISTIC PERIOD

No other example is known
of a Hellenistic vase-shaped
earring in the form of a
loutrophoros, a ceremonial
vessel used for nuptial baths
and placed on the grave of an
unmarried person. While
this piece was purportedly
found with the rest of the
Thessalian Treasure (see plates
29, 30, 32 & 33), in style it is
earlier than the 2nd century
B.C., indicating either that the
earring was not part of the
horde, or perhaps that it was a
family heirloom surviving
from an earlier time or made
in an earlier mode.

PLATE 32
Ring with intaglio Nike
HELLENISTIC PERIOD

The carnelian in the center of
the bezel of this ring has an
intaglio representation of Nike,
the Greek goddess of victory,
driving a two-horse chariot.
She holds the reins and a goad
in her right hand, and a wreath
of victory in her upraised left
hand. The style of the figure
is close to a number of late 3rd
and early 2nd-century B.C.
gemstones.

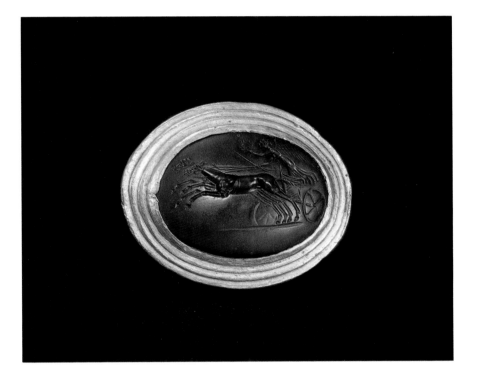

PLATE 33
Ring with intaglio bezel
HELLENISTIC PERIOD

Greek seal rings displayed
personal or symbolic devices.
An intaglio design on a seal
like this one would appear in
raised relief when pressed
onto soft wax or clay. The
interesting scene of a reclining
nude woman with a swan
seems to refer to Leda, who
was seduced by Zeus in the
guise of a swan. There are,
however, unusual features in
the scene, including a satyr and
arms and armor in addition to
the swan. Possibly, the woman
is Aphrodite and the armor
indicates Ares, god of war.

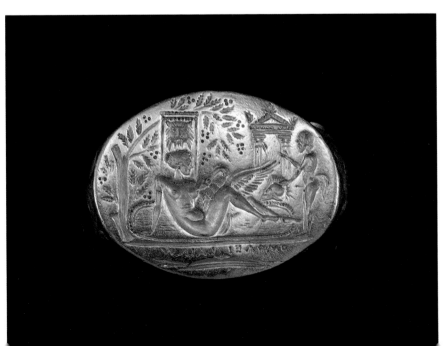

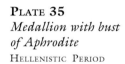

PLATE 34
*Pair of earrings
with doves*
HELLENISTIC PERIOD

Naturalistic representations
using colored stones, like
this pair of doves, were manu-
factured from the 3rd century
B.C. on. The treatment of
the doves demonstrates the
way in which a large colored
component, once only an
ornament, came to be used
as the background for other
ornaments, forming a rich
interplay of gold and colored
stone. Doves were symbols
of love, faithfulness and
conjugal devotion.

PLATE 35
*Medallion with bust
of Aphrodite*
HELLENISTIC PERIOD

The bust of Aphrodite,
goddess of love, is modelled
in very high relief against a
round sheet gold disc. Over
her shoulder peers a youthful,
winged Eros. Originally, the
medallion was worn as a
pendant attached to a chain
and may have been a good
luck charm. The finely
executed female head and
the striking contrast between
red garnet and green glass
inlay reflects a later Hellenistic
taste for decorative effects.

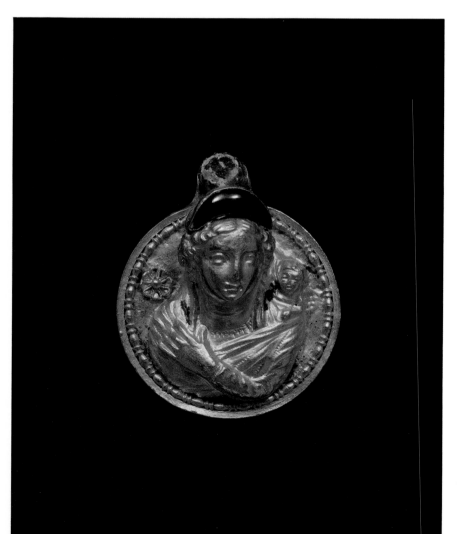

PLATE 36
*Pair of earrings with
erotes and masks*
HELLENISTIC PERIOD

Flying *erotes* lift their arms
above their heads, holding a
mask in their hands. The type
of Eros with a bare belly,
derived from the Near Eastern
fertility deity Attis, is standard
in late Hellenistic gold jewelry.
Such figures occur in vase
paintings and theater scenes
also. The baroque exuberance
of colored gems set in high
bezels with pearls is typical of
the late Hellenistic world.

PLATE 37
*Pair of erotes earrings
with Isis crowns*
HELLENISTIC PERIOD

These *erotes* are cast in solid
gold and are surmounted by
garnets and Isis crowns with
emeralds. The drinking vessels
and amphoras held by the
erotes indicate the jollity of
a Dionysiac drinking scene,
while the Isis crown, a
common decorative finial in
late Hellenistic work, stems
from Egyptian jewelry. This
type of earring was worn with
the loop-in-loop chain in front.

PLATE 38
Medallion with Eros
HELLENISTIC PERIOD

The figure of a naked Eros, standing on a base, is embossed on an oval sheet gold plaque. In one hand the little boy holds a club, in the other a quiver and arrows, indicating that the youthful deity is armed with weapons stolen from the demigod, Herakles. Love, the all-powerful child, was a very popular theme in Hellenistic art and may be found in bas-reliefs as well as jewelry.

PLATE 39
Snake ring
HELLENISTIC PERIOD

In a very three-dimensional design, this ring consists of four medallions linked by wires and ornamented with emeralds and carnelians. Round wires soldered to the ring terminate in two pairs of snake heads, poised as if to strike. Such lively works, enriched by polychromy, date to the 1st century B.C.

PLATE 40
Pair of bracelets
HELLENISTIC PERIOD

Snake bracelets are known as early as the Geometric Period, but became more common during Archaic and Classical times and reached a height of popularity in the Hellenistic Age. In the cosmopolitan Hellenistic kingdoms, emphasis was placed on the serpent's talismanic power, which was associated with the sacred *uraeus* cobra of Egypt. Although paintings of women wearing such bracelets are common in the Roman Empire, stylistically these examples are probably Hellenistic.

THE ROMAN PERIOD

During the third and second centuries B.C., neither the centers of the Hellenistic World like Pergamon, Antioch and Alexandria, nor the confederacies of states in mainland Greece, succeeded in re-establishing the kingdom of Alexander the Great or returning to the classical *polis.* Instead, the growing power of Rome led to the eventual conquest of Greek lands by the Roman Republic. By the late first century B.C., Rome ruled an empire that stretched across the entire Mediterranean. However, the Greek world under Roman rule continued its cultural dominion. The Romans adopted Greek philosophy, literature and art as educational models. Within the lands of the vast Roman Empire, Hellenism acquired an ecumenical character, forming a common culture for Europe, Asia and Africa. Old classical city-states like Athens or Corinth and Hellenistic centers like Miletos, Ephesos or Alexandria did very well economically under the Roman state. As a consequence, jewelry continued to be a primary means of secular display (*fig. 22*).

The Romans of the early Republic had scorned jewelry as effeminate and demoralizing, but the sophisticated Romans of the Empire adopted Greek jewelry techniques and encouraged the production of fashionable ornaments stemming from the luxurious workshops of Alexandria or Antioch. Jewelry of the Roman period continues Hellenistic traditions, with a gradual simplification of forms (*fig. 23*).

Fig. 22
Oak wreath
Roman Period
(opposite)

Fig. 23
Snake bracelet
Roman Period

FIG. 24
Bracelet
ROMAN PERIOD

Filigree and granulation were used less extensively, as the display of precious and semi-precious stones, including pearls, became more popular (*fig. 24*). The widespread use of jewelry during the Empire is readily seen in the series of portraits of distinguished people from the Fayum in Egypt. In these paintings, necklaces, earrings, pendants, and bracelets are faithfully reproduced. From the late second century A.D. on, a popular Roman ornamental device was the use of coins with imperial portraits as decorative elements (*see plate 49*). During the third century a new gold-working technique, which was to have a long future, was introduced. This *opus interrasile* work produced decorative motifs by perforating gold leaf (*fig. 25*).

The sophisticated tradition of Roman jewelry (*fig. 26*) passed without a significant change into Christian Byzantine art. Jewelry at Constantinople continued to fulfill the purpose of classical ornament, which was to exhibit the beauty, status and sensual allure of noble women and to provide rich visual symbols for church and state.

FIG. 25
Bracelet
ROMAN PERIOD

FIG. 26
*Garnet ring with intaglio
of horseman and foe*
ROMAN PERIOD

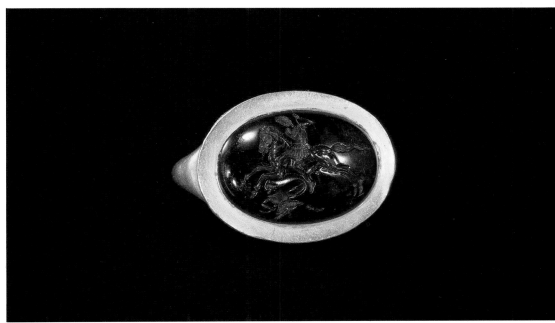

PLATE 41
Ivy wreath
ROMAN PERIOD
(opposite)

Greek wreaths were worn in
processions and as symbols of
victory; they were also buried
with the dead, as a sign of
victory in life. Naturalistic
wreaths like this one, depicting
ivy stem, leaves and berries, go
back to the 4th century B.C.,
but unusual details such as the
device on the stem, or the
shape of the leaves, suggest a
late Hellenistic or Roman date.

PLATE 42
Snake ring
ROMAN PERIOD

The development of snake
rings parallels that of snake
bracelets. Examples are
common in the Roman period,
the jewelry of which generally
continued Hellenistic Greek
traditions and often employed
Greek craftsmen. Such rings
might be decorated with
precious stones or, as here,
ornamented with chasing to
indicate the snake's scales.
The stylized elegance of this
ring probably dates to the late
1st century B.C. or the 1st
century A.D.

PLATE 43
Pair of bracelets with
Isis and Serapis
ROMAN PERIOD

Hinged bracelets, in which one
end serves as a pin to unfasten
the bracelet's centerpiece, were
produced from the late
Hellenistic period until the 3rd
century A.D. Examples with
figurative imagery like this one
are rare. The Egyptian deities
Isis and Serapis are shown as
human to the waist and as
serpents below. The serpents'
coils are entwined in a Knot of
Herakles, which probably refers
to the Greek myth that Zeus
and his mother Rhea mated in
the guise of snakes. Other
indications of talismanic powers
are the cornucopia and offering
bowl held by the figures, the
measuring cup of agricultural
fertility crowning them, and
the Dionysiac basket of poppies
and wheat between them.

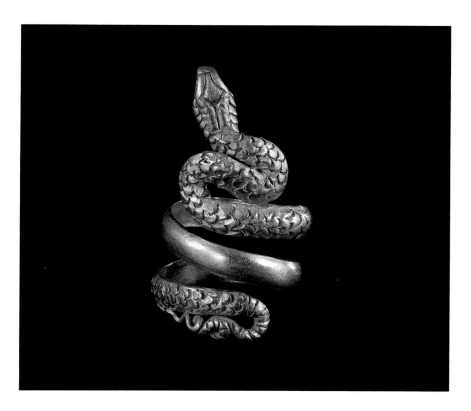

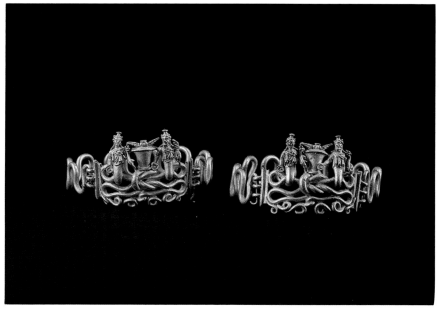

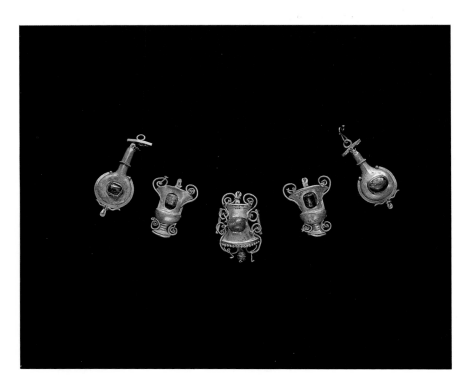

PLATE 44
Set of gold pendants for a necklace
ROMAN PERIOD

During the Roman Period an expanding range of jewelry styles emphasized colored stones and sheet gold. These highly baroque pendants, in the form of drinking cups, a flask and a vase, all display associations with Dionysos, god of wine. The original necklace would have had rows of beads or knots to separate the pendants and additional decoration on the pendants of pearls or glass beads. The pendants were found in a woman's grave in Piraeus, the port of Athens, along with several other pieces in the Benaki collections.

PLATE 45
Rock crystal amulets
ROMAN PERIOD

Other fine objects from the Piraeus grave are these rock crystal amulets in the shape of a shell, a duck, a tortoise, and two fish. Roman rock crystal came from sources as far apart as India, the Alps and Portugal. Given the rarity of the stone, it is not surprising to find that bits left over from the manufacture of large works like vases were later used for jewelry. As all but the shell in this set are pierced, the talismans may have been strung on a necklace.

Plate 46
Snake head bracelet
Roman Period

While snake bracelets were very popular in antiquity, double-headed ones are less common. In this example, the scales are clearly and naturalistically represented in low relief, while the heads, which were made separately and fitted onto the body hoop, have glass eyes and glass gem pomegranates in their mouths. The popularity of snake bracelets reflects a strong connection with the mystery religions, such as the cult of the Egyptian goddess, Isis, or that of Dionysos Sabazios, in which snakes were important symbols of fertility, power and the afterlife.

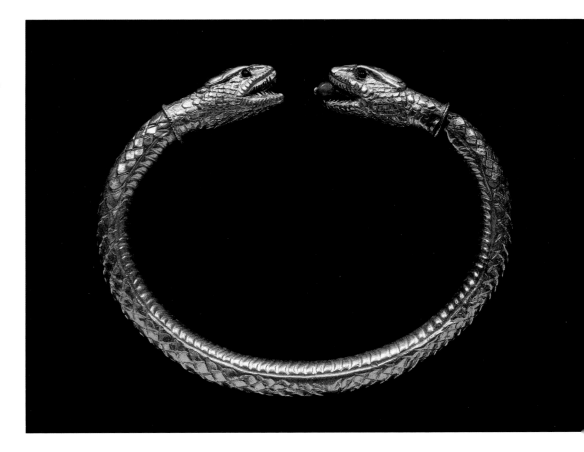

Plate 47
Ring with engraved agate
Roman Period

Images on Roman gems range from portraits of emperors and private individuals to representations of Greek gods and heroes. This banded agate ring is engraved in intaglio with a scene of the Greek hero Menelaos rescuing the dead body of the young Patroklos on the field of battle, a very dramatic moment in Book 17 of the *Iliad*. The composition is known from several Roman marble sculptures, thought to be copies of a 3rd century B.C. Greek bronze original. The abundance of versions in the Roman imperial period attests to the popularity of a story stressing heroic fidelity to the dead.

PLATE 48
Necklace with Medusa medallion and bust of Isis
ROMAN PERIOD

From a loop-in-loop chain made of bent gold wire rings is suspended a gold disc, to which is soldered a Medusa head in relief. The Medusa, who is of the "beautiful woman" type, has wings and snakes in her hair, with the ends of the snakes knotted under her chin. Halfway along the chain is a pendant with a relief bust of Isis, which suggests that the owner of the necklace was an initiate of the Isis cult, an Egyptian religion known in Athens since classical times. Both the Medusa and the Isis were thought to be talismans against the evil eye.

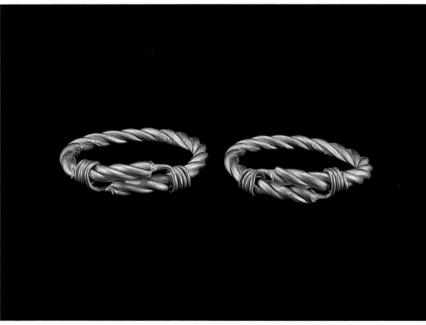

PLATE 49
Pair of bracelets
ROMAN PERIOD

These bracelets are made of two twisted gold wires, forming a hoop with overlapping ends. Each end of the hoop slides back and forth through the wound wires, so that the bracelet could be adjusted to fit different wrist sizes. This example probably dates to the 3rd century A.D.

PLATE 50
Chain with pendant
ROMAN PERIOD

The pendant has a coin of
the emperor Hadrian set in a
round mount, which is
decorated with a series of
pierced palmettes, and is hung
from a closely-meshed gold
link chain. There are similar
examples of pendant-mounted
coins from the first half of the
3rd century A.D., a period
in which unsettled political
conditions in the Roman
Empire led to mounting
coins in jewelry as a way of
hording money. The style of
the pendant mount ultimately
derives from Hellenistic
work, showing how long
these Eastern Mediterranean
traditions lasted in the Empire.

PLATE 51
Bracelet
ROMAN PERIOD

This bracelet consists of a
hoop of hammered-out thick
silver wire with overlapping
ends, forged into round wire.
The ends are wound loosely
around the hoop so as to make
it adjustable. Such bracelets
were common in Egypt in the
later Roman period.

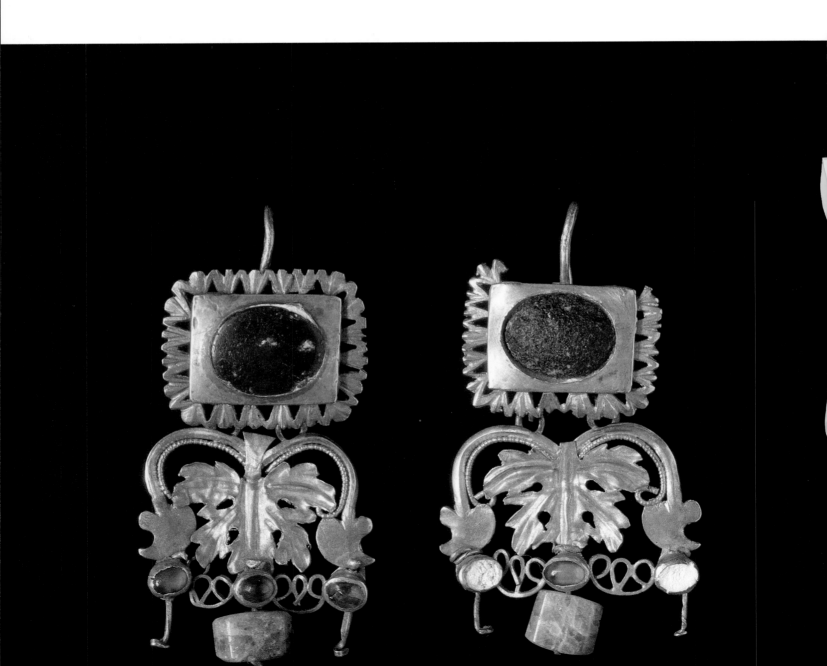

When the Emperor Constantine the Great moved the capital of
the Roman Empire from Rome to Constantinople in 324 A.D.,
he was determined to make this ancient Greek colony of Byzantium
into the greatest city in the world. Many new monumental
buildings were erected beside the Golden Horn and ancient works
of art were assembled to beautify the new town. Thus the art of
the Byzantine Empire began as a continuation of the traditions
of Greco-Roman culture. In this enterprise gold and silversmiths
participated. The imperial court lavishly patronized workers in
precious metals, and skills developed at the wealthy Greek cities of
Alexandria and Antioch were used in the development of Byzantine
style. Like Athens and Rome in earlier centuries, Constantinople
was the center of a great trading network, which produced
enormous wealth for the imperial city. The conversion of the
empire to Christianity in the fourth century A.D. meant an
enrichment of the themes of art, without a loss of Greco-Roman
techniques or typology.

Whether pagan or Christian in inspiration, fourth century Byzantine
jewelry was abstract and decorative in character (*fig. 27*). This
character was accentuated in the later Roman Empire by economic
difficulties, which temporarily led to a decline in supplies of gold and
gemstones. More thrifty techniques, such as pierced decoration or
the use of thin sheets of gold foil, replaced massive displays of
precious jewels. The predominate motifs were delicate stems and
tendrils, so fine they could pass for filigree.

With the improvement in Byzantine wealth and power from the fifth
century A.D. on, luxurious taste began to reappear in jewelry. The
age of the Emperor Justinian, especially, represented a balance of
Greek and Christian elements in an art that was both mystical and
humanist. Scenes in the Ravenna mosaics of Justinian, the Empress
Theodora and their court show the imperial entourage decked in

FIG. 27
Pair of earrings
EARLY BYZANTINE PERIOD

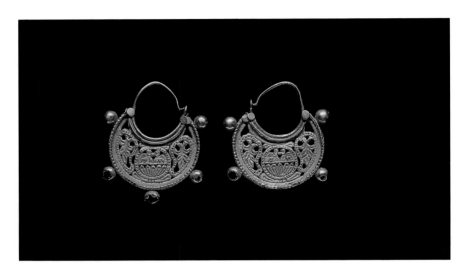

FIG. 28
Pair of earrings
EARLY BYZANTINE PERIOD

sumptuous gold jewelry and blazing with precious stones. Some types of ornament, such as necklaces threaded with sapphires, hexagonal emeralds and pearls, may be found from Tunis and Rome to Constantinople, demonstrating the extent of Byzantine power and influence. The slightly later lunate earrings with facing peacocks (*fig. 28*) are found all over the Mediterranean world. Many of these works are as fine in their miniature style as contemporary Byzantine painting, sculpture or mosaic. Like the fine arts, jewelry indicates that throughout the sixth and early seventh centuries Constantinople remained a source of fashionable design across the Mediterranean (*fig. 29*).

FIG. 29
Pair of earrings
EARLY BYZANTINE PERIOD

Much early Byzantine jewelry depicts Christian themes, prominently incorporating figures of the Virgin, Christ, holy saints or the Christian cross (*fig. 30*). In style and technique these early Byzantine works are still based on Greco-Roman work and continue its central concern with naturalistic representations of the human figure.

FIG. 30
Ring
Early Byzantine Period

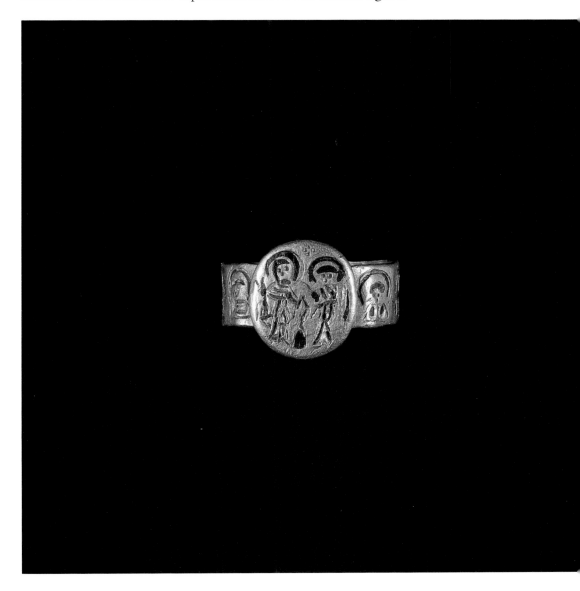

PLATE 52
Section of a necklace
EARLY BYZANTINE PERIOD

Three of the sections of this necklace, which came from a treasure found in Alexandria, Egypt, are composite pendants of emerald, sapphire and pearl mounted on raised ornamental supports, which reflect light upon the gemstones. Connecting these pendants are box-like settings with carnelians. This concentration on the gem rather than the goldwork creates a design of great opulence and imaginativeness. It may fairly be called one of the most important surviving pieces of Byzantine gold jewelry from the 5th century A.D.

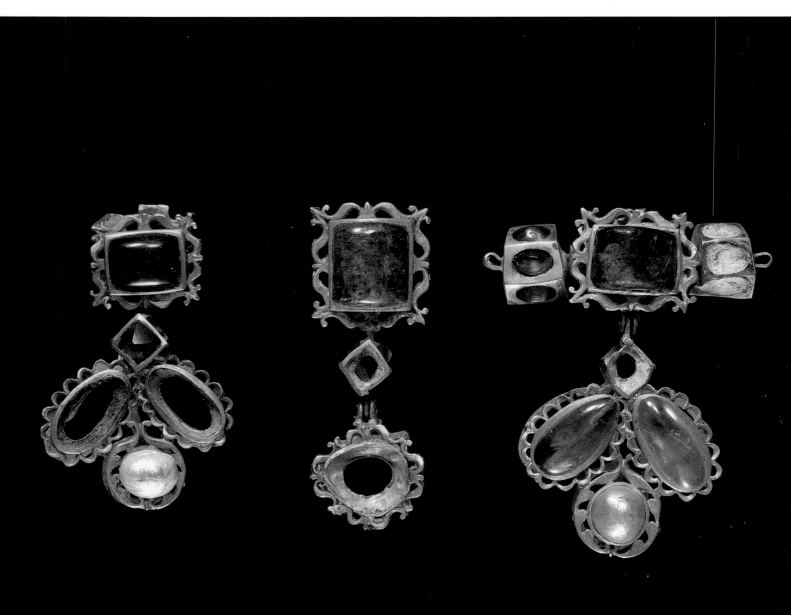

PLATE 53
Necklace
EARLY BYZANTINE PERIOD

Beads of sapphires, amethysts,
emeralds and pearls are
threaded on this gold chain.
Similar necklaces have been
found buried with their owners
during the troubled invasion
period of the 5th century A.D.
Judging by the pictures of the
Empress Theodora in the
Ravenna mosaics, such
necklaces were a basic item of
jewelry for the imperial court
and great Byzantine aristocrats
in the 5th and 6th centuries.
The abundant use of precious
gemstones also testifies to
extensive Byzantine trade
with the East, especially India
and Ceylon.

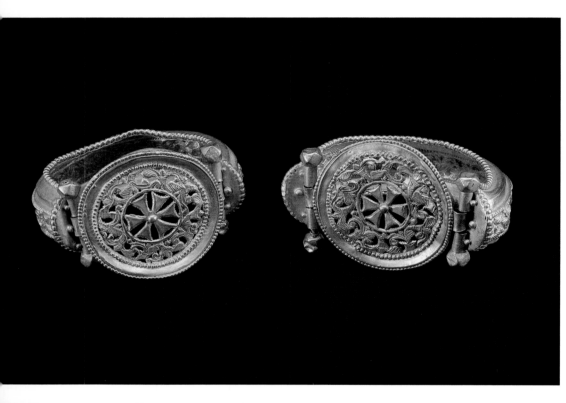

PLATE 54
Pair of bracelets
EARLY BYZANTINE PERIOD

These bracelets consist of a band of semi-circular section embossed with a decoration of tendrils sprouting from a cornucopia and a moveable disc with the same tendril motifs perforated around a star-like rosette. One bracelet is probably earlier in date than the other, as the ornament is superior and more defined. This style of ornamentation is found on sculptured reliefs from the late 6th century A.D. Contemporary representations show how widely these bracelets with hinged discs were used by ladies of the Byzantine court.

PLATE 55
Bracelet clasp
EARLY BYZANTINE PERIOD

The monogram on this bracelet clasp, -**EAo** in niello, indicates a date in the second half of the 6th century A.D. It is difficult to establish what sort of bracelet the clasp bound. Treasures surviving from the period include bracelets with tubular hoops flattened at the top, which were bound by similar clasps. The monogram may refer to Gillo, a magical dragon spirit that attacked women in childbirth, indicating that the clasp was a talisman to avert evil.

PLATE 56
Ring
EARLY BYZANTINE PERIOD

In the early years of Christianity, the Church Fathers discouraged the wearing of jewelry, but they did allow rings to be worn, either a signet ring or a wedding ring. For signets, Christian symbols like anchors, fish or birds were common, though in the course of time these motifs were superseded by monograms. This example was probably a signet ring belonging to a consul, for the eagle was a sign of authority. The fact that the eagle is combined with a monogram of a man's name also indicates a titled owner. However, the eagle has other possible biblical associations, too.

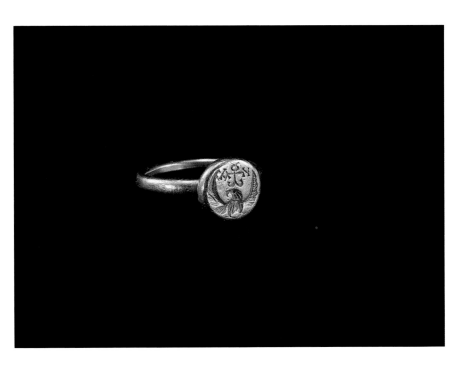

PLATE 57
Ring
EARLY BYZANTINE PERIOD

A quatrefoil calyx bezel is attached to the semicircular hoop of this ring. The center of the bezel may have contained a relic, a gemstone, or an inset of glass paste. It is also possible that the ring was an unfinished blank. The design is clearly meant to suggest a cross, indicating that the ring was intended as a protective amulet.

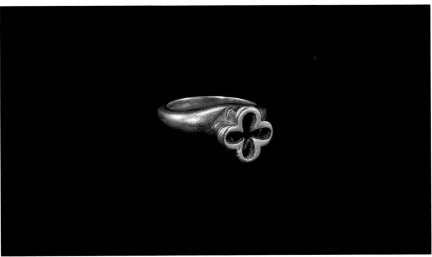

PLATE 58
Swivel ring
EARLY BYZANTINE PERIOD

The bezel of this ring is octagonal, with an incised representation of a standing archangel holding in his right hand a cross-scepter and in the other a globe. On the other face of the bezel is a representation of St. Thekla flanked by lions. The cryptograms on the thickness of the bezel are shorthand symbols for Christian prayers. Swivel rings are unusual in the Byzantine period; this example probably comes from Syria or Cilicia, as the cult of St. Thekla centered in Cilicia.

PLATE 59
Cross
EARLY BYZANTINE PERIOD

This cross consists of flaring
tubular arms made of gold
foil, with an attached quatrefoil rosette at the center. It
is a common type and has
been found in various
treasure hordes of the early
7th century A.D.

PLATE 60
Buckle with belt plate
Early Byzantine Period

The silver buckle has an elliptical rim and a hinged, drop-shaped tongue, while the belt plate is lyre-shaped with a cable border. There are many comparable examples of this common type of buckle. From the broad proportions and block monogram, the piece probably dates to the end of the 6th century A.D.

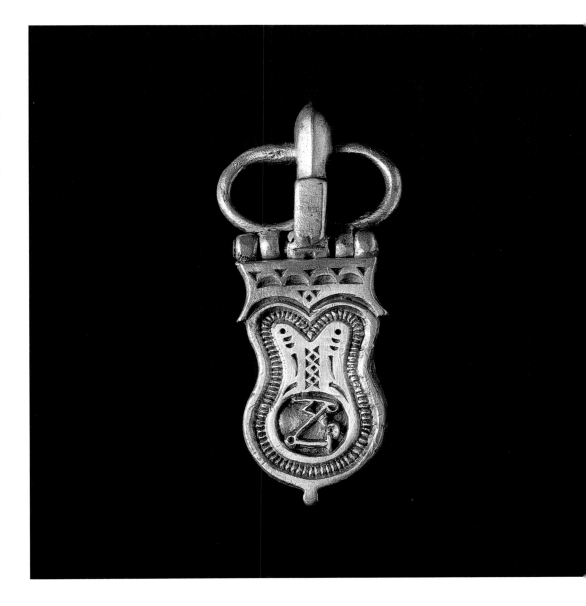

THE LATER BYZANTINE EMPIRE

he eighth century A.D. was a watershed for Byzantine Greek culture. Assaulted by the expanding Arabs from outside, the Byzantine Empire was racked within by the Iconoclastic Controversy. This religious conflict centered on the value of images and questioned the importance Greco-Roman art had given to representations of the human figure. The warfare and cultural upheaval associated with this controversy left a mark on the art of jewelry. Much of the gold that had formerly been in use went out of circulation. Treasure troves were buried frequently in these troubled times, providing valuable evidence for the abrupt decline in jewelry production during the eighth and ninth centuries.

By the late ninth century, the Empire had begun to recover from this prolonged crisis. With the advent of the Macedonian dynasty (867-1056 A.D.), there was a new stability in political and cultural life. Byzantium once again embarked on a "universalist" policy, which combined the Greek tradition and the Orthodox Christian faith. Work in all artistic fields, from manuscript illumination and ikon painting to textiles and goldwork, reflected the high standards of taste achieved by this revived naturalistic art (*fig. 31, fig. 32*).

FIG. 31
Reliquary cross
LATER BYZANTINE PERIOD
(opposite)

FIG. 32
*Reliquary cross with
inner cross*
LATER BYZANTINE PERIOD

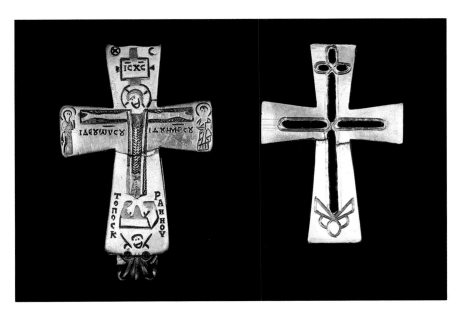

A distinctive characteristic of the jewelry of this period is the use of enamel, which was employed to manufacture exquisite miniature works (*fig. 33*). Wealth and opulence appear in the use of precious stones on royal gifts, church plate and personal jewelry. Liturgical pieces often exemplify the profound spirituality which informs Middle Byzantine art. Goldsmiths and enamel makers produced glowing miniature scenes on church plate, which expressed a triumphant Christian faith. In personal jewelry, delicate work like filigree or cameo was popular. The inclusion of Christian symbolism in this jewelry indicates that the pieces were used for amulets.

Another critical watershed for the Byzantine Empire was the sack of Constantinople by Western Christian crusaders in 1204 A.D. The pillaging of treasures in the capital and the domination of the state by Latin Christians from Western Europe meant the destruction of

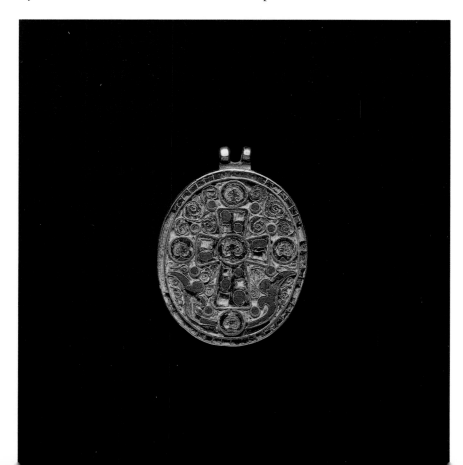

FIG. 33
Oval plaque with hinge/suspension-lugs
LATER BYZANTINE PERIOD

Fig. 34
Pectoral cross
Later Byzantine Period

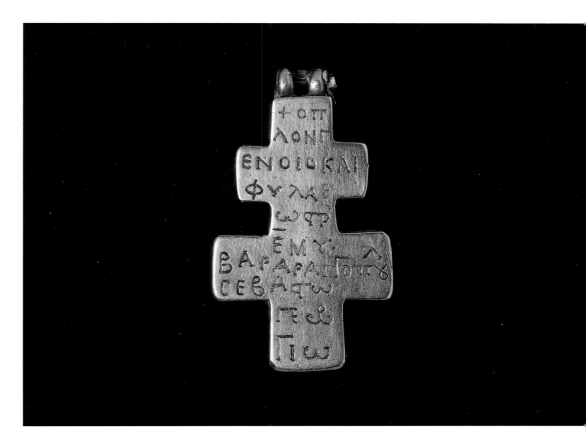

over a thousand years of accumulated art work. Jewelry, particularly, suffered in these difficult times. Although the Paleologus dynasty (1260-1453) succeeded in re-establishing Byzantine power, the lands of the empire were fragmented and constantly under attack from groups of Islamic Turks. These final centuries of Byzantine rule ended with the capture of Constantinople by the Ottoman Turks in 1453 A.D.

The Greeks, on the defensive everywhere in the late Middle Ages, had little time or wealth to spend on sumptuary art. In the last stages of Byzantine jewelry, the poverty of precious materials was compensated for by technical proficiency (*fig. 34*). Great advances were made in filigree work, while the delicate decorative designs on liturgical vessels and jewelry were now more often than not made of silver rather than gold.

PLATE 61
Reliquary cross
MIDDLE BYZANTINE PERIOD

The two symmetrical sections
of this pectoral cross and
reliquary are joined by hinges
covered with palmettes. Inside
the outer cross was a smaller
cross designed to hold a relic
of the True Cross. The cross is
decorated with incised designs
and niello inlay, showing scenes
of the Crucifixion on the front
and the Virgin on the back.
Niello reliquaries of this type
seem to have been common
from the 9th or 10th century
A.D. onwards in Constantinople, as well as in other parts
of the Empire. The method
of niello inlay suggests an
11th century date.

PLATE 62
Bracelet
MIDDLE BYZANTINE PERIOD

The sections of this broad, cylindrical, gilded-silver bracelet are each decorated with a repoussé roundel framed by four almond shapes. The design on the roundels, picked out with a thin layer of niello, consists of a cross formed by four scrolled palmettes. This design is a simplified version of ornamental bracelets, both Byzantine and Islamic, derived from the ornaments of Sassanid Persia. Persian decorative styles were transmitted to the West by way of luxury fabrics, ceramics and metalwork.

PLATES 63, 64
Medusa amulet
MIDDLE BYZANTINE PERIOD

On one side of the silver amulet is a woman's head in low relief, whose snake hair terminates in lion heads. The design represents a blending of the classical image of the gorgon Medusa with the Egyptian protective deity Chnoubis, who appeared as a lion-headed serpent. On the reverse side is a magical inscription. Such ornamental charms were medico-magical amulets, whose form and function goes back to classical antiquity. The inscription relates to childbirth and the use of silver, rather than gold, indicates a woman's amulet, perhaps one designed for the Christian pilgrim trade in the Near East.

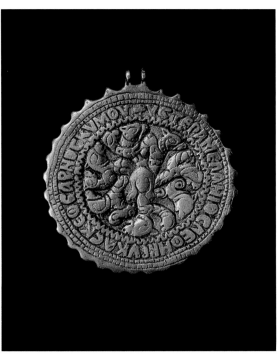

PLATE 65
Encolpium
MIDDLE BYZANTINE PERIOD
(opposite)

The carving of hard gemstones, like this rock crystal medallion, was a sumptuous art which Byzantium inherited from Hellenistic and Roman times. These jewels were made into small pendants called *encolpia*, which depicted religious subjects, or were used as inset ornaments for gospel covers, diadems and other articles. The Benaki cameo of Christ Pantokrator ("Lord of All") seems to have been set originally in a larger object. The present gilt silver mount set with rubies, emeralds and pearls probably dates to the 16th century, when a Byzantine treasure of the 11th century would have been a precious heirloom.

PLATE 66
Earring
MIDDLE BYZANTINE

Very elaborate openwork and filigree ornamentation covers this basket-shaped earring, with many details picked out in finely granulated wire. While the piece is modelled on Early Christian basket earrings, it is far more complex, with a density and variety of decoration covering the whole surface of the earring in a manner that suggests Oriental influence.

PLATE 67
Pectoral cross
LATE BYZANTINE PERIOD

This small gold cross of the Resurrection type was made from three pieces of sheet gold soldered together in a three-dimensional form. Inset in the front is a lapis lazuli cross embedded in its own protective case. The two-armed Resurrection type of cross is associated with reliquaries which were designed to hold a piece of the True Cross. On the reverse of the cross, an inscription gives the name of the owner, a Varangopoulos, who was probably descended from the Varangians, foreign mercenaries who formed the Byzantine Emperor's personal bodyguard.

On the 29th of May 1453, the Ottoman Turks captured Constantinople, ending a more than thousand year tradition of Greek sovereignty. Yet the Greek world never abandoned its faith in the continuity of the Byzantine heritage. For the next four hundred years this heritage left its imprint on the spiritual life, culture and creative endeavors of the Christian Greek-speaking peoples.

In the western parts of Greece, in Crete and in the islands of the Ionian Sea, where Greeks had been living under Latin domination since the Fourth Crusade, a reasonably high level of trade and prosperity continued throughout the Post-Byzantine centuries, with Venice replacing Constantinople as a dominant trading power in the Aegean area. A great artist like El Greco came from this mixed cultural background. Western influences are obvious in both art and jewelry. A long-lived example of western taste in ornament is the profusion of boat-shaped earrings to be found everywhere in this area (*fig. 35*).

In the parts of Greece under Turkish domination, life was much harder, with warfare, pillage and enslavement common occurrences. Consequently, while western European artistic ideas filtered into the Venetian-controlled areas of Greece, the eastern parts of the Greek world were cut off from greater European developments. The art

FIG. 35
Pectoral in the shape of a four-masted sailing boat
POST-BYZANTINE PERIOD
(opposite)

FIG. 36
Head ornament with chains and pendants
POST-BYZANTINE PERIOD

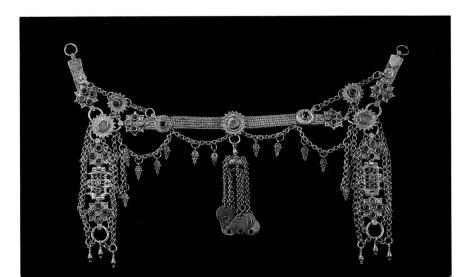

of mainland Greece under the Ottomans seems to represent a more direct continuation of the Byzantine tradition. Some of the surviving pieces of jewelry might actually be mistaken for works of the Late Byzantine period, were it not for the inscriptions of a later date. Seventeenth century Greek jewelry is characterized by an imposing quality, reminiscent of the imperial past of the East, rather than the more graceful style of the seventeenth-century West

FIG. 37
Pendant (back view)
POST-BYZANTINE PERIOD

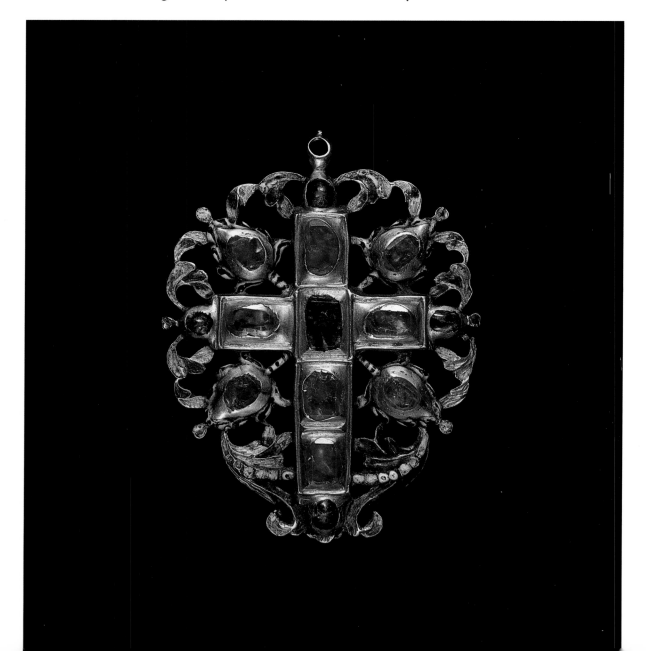

FIG. 38
Pendant (front view)
POST-BYZANTINE PERIOD

(*fig. 36*). The almost exclusive use of silver is a sign of difficult economic times, although the upper class and churchmen continued to wear gold jewelry, which was largely imported from abroad. Surviving examples of 18th century jewelry adorned with enamel and precious stones seem to have been largely made in Constantinople (*fig. 37, fig. 38*). Little scholarly work has been done on the jewelry of this period, but it is clearly more than simply "folk art."

PLATE 68
Pendant
(opposite)

This pendant represents a rare combination of techniques, including an imitation of cloisonné enamel and filigree decoration, post-Byzantine iconography, and a Renaissance foliage mounting. Unlike Renaissance filigree enamel techniques in the west, the Benaki pendant uses empty filigree decoration, which is only filled with enamel on the face of the Virgin. The agate from which the pendant was made was probably considered a gem with mystic properties, and therefore was worthy to be offered to the Holy Abbess Theophano, who is mentioned in the inscription.

PLATE 69
Caravel earrings

Earrings with ship pendants belong to a larger group of ornaments, which were called *Venetika* ("Venetian") in 17th century Greece. Despite this fact, and the appearance of Venice's Lion of St. Mark on the caravel's flag, it is possible that this type of jewelry was made somewhere in the Greek islands, at a center open to Western European influences. The earrings are notable for highly coloristic effects achieved by the contrast of filigree enamel, pearls and gold.

PLATE 70
Necklace
Post-Byzantine Period
(opposite)

Originally, such necklaces were probably much larger, hanging down to the wearer's waist, but the Greek custom whereby a mother divided family jewels among her daughters led to a reduction in size. Often these "chain necklaces" ended in costly pendants in the shape of eagles or caravels. The character of the Western-style miniatures attached to the necklace and the lesser importance of enamel in the design indicate a date in the mid-18th century.

PLATE 71
Dangle earrings
Post-Byzantine Period

These sumptuous earrings consist of an elaborate series of pendants made of gold foil with pierced decoration and filigree work. They are the largest and most impressive of four pairs from the island of Kos, now in the Benaki Museum. Called *kambanes*, the type could still be seen on Kos in the early years of this century. Originally, the earrings would have been part of a set of head gear which included a frontlet, and which would frame the face in a manner reminiscent of Byzantine head ornaments.

PLATE 72
Three pendants from a pectoral ornament
Post-Byzantine Period

Three pendants, strung on a chain of later date, form part of a pectoral ornament called a *kadena*, traditionally part of a bridal costume on the Island of Corfu. The two cross-shaped pendants framing the central rosette pendant are worked in fine filigree and set with pearls. The central pendant was probably once garnished with polychrome enamel and pearls. Since such pendants were kept as heirlooms and reworked into various kinds of wedding jewelry, they need not have formed a group originally.

PLATE 73
Torque
POST-BYZANTINE PERIOD
(opposite)

This rare type of choker consists of a silver hoop twisted like a rope, hence the name "torque." This one is threaded with polyhedral beads, rivetted rosettes, swivelling pieces in the form of birds and a rectangular central ornament. The decoration imitates granulation and filigree work and there are gems in clawtooth settings, as well as the incised date of 1691. The style of the piece, which probably comes from North Greece, has strong connections with medieval Byzantine work.

PLATES 74, 75
Panaghiarion
POST-BYZANTINE PERIOD

A *panaghiarion* is used in the Christian liturgy as a receptacle for the Virgin's portion of the eucharistic bread. The "Elevation of the Panaghia" occurs on special occasions, such as imperial dinners in the Byzantine Period, or for monks' formal meals in Greek monasteries. Originally a shallow dish, the *panaghiarion* became a Bishop's pendant. The Benaki example, which belonged to the 17th-century Metropolitan Neophytos of Nicomedia, consists of two ivory discs in silver mountings, with niello inscriptions. The figurative scenes, which include the Virgin praying and Abraham with an angel, are surrounded by medallions with various biblical and liturgical images. These intricate scenes relate to monumental paintings of the Tree of Jesse, the genealogy of Christ.

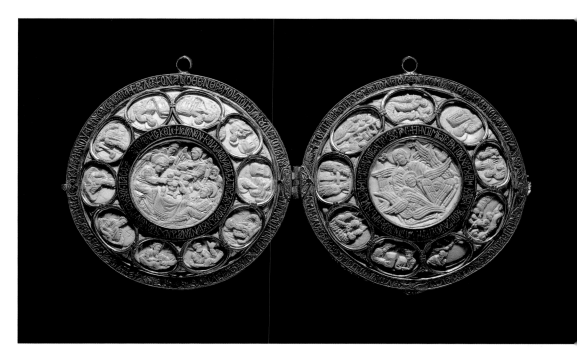

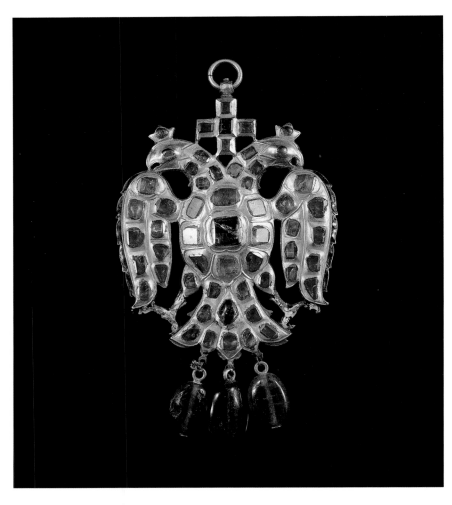

PLATES 76, 77
Ecclesiastical pectoral
POST-BYZANTINE PERIOD

Besides their function as an amulet, precious hieratic pectorals symbolized the prestige of both the prelate who wore the jewelry and the Greek Orthodox Church. The presence of a double-headed eagle in this piece signifies the secular power of ecclesiastical authority after the Fall of Constantinople in 1453 A.D. Stylistically, the pectoral owes much to Ottoman Turkish jewelry, while the enamel paintings of the Virgin and Christ, the Annunciation, and the Crucifixion, are European in character. The delicate blue and pink enamels reflect the work of Genoese craftsmen employed in Constantinople.

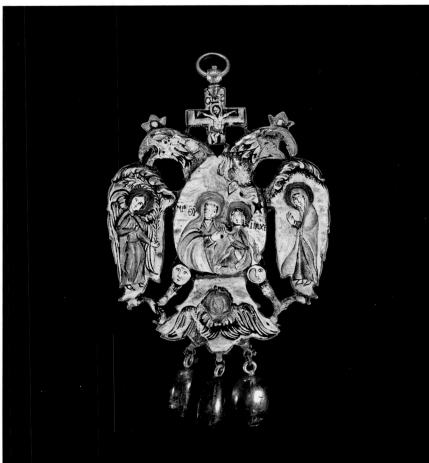

PLATES 78, 79
*Pectoral of the
patriarch Parthenios*
POST-BYZANTINE PERIOD

The impression left by this
jewel is that it is of European,
rather than Ottoman,
inspiration, though it was
made in Constantinople. The
technique of enamel painting
used to depict scenes of the
Holy Trinity, Christ, angels,
cherubs, symbols of the
evangelists and the Heavenly
Powers, as well as the foliate
settings of the stones, the
palmettes, and the cartouches
with rococo scrolls, all reveal
European taste. Byzantine
and Western iconography
are blended in the images on
the reverse. The owner of the
pectoral, Parthenios Gavalas,
from the island of Santorini,
was a distinguished prelate
who rose to be Metropolitan
of the Greek Church in
Constantinople. He belonged
to an aristocratic family
and became a scholar and
connoisseur of the arts.

B y the second half of the eighteenth century, the heartland of
Greece had become more prosperous. From a country of
farmers, herders and small artisans, living a repressed life under
Turkish rule, the Greek people turned to shipping and trade for
greater economic possibilities. Coastal towns and the islands grew
into maritime centers, while the Greek merchant fleet became an
important factor in Mediterranean trade. All these events stimulated
the cultural flowering known as the Neo-Hellenic Enlightenment,
which was to lead eventually to the Greek War of Independence.

Neo-Hellenic art of the late eighteenth century was a synthesis
of past traditions, including the austere grandeur of Byzantine art,
the decorative designs of Islamic art, with its foliate motifs and
counterpoint of flowers, several influences from Western art, and,
finally, the uniform style established among the Greek-speaking
peoples of the Ottoman Empire (*fig. 39*). Like local folk costumes,
Neo-Hellenic jewelry had many interesting regional variants, with
individual characteristics as marked as dialects. Common features
shared by all these folk traditions were leaf-shaped pendants, which
tinkled when the wearer moved (*fig. 40*), and floral elements

Fig. 39
Belt buckle
Neo-Hellenic Period
(opposite)

Fig. 40
*Silver choker with
pendant coins*
Neo-Hellenic Period

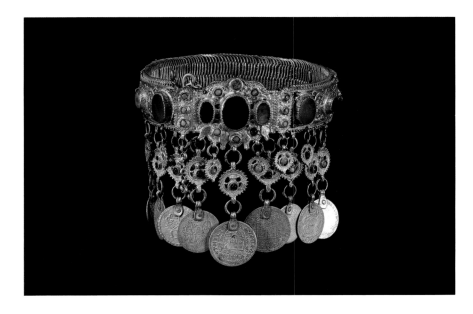

symbolizing fertility and the adornment of brides. Apotropaic and protective amulets included the double-headed eagle, the human head and the cross. Pendants often included coins, which earlier had been used as a means of saving wealth, but which were purely decorative by the early nineteenth century (*fig. 41*). The character of Neo-Hellenic metal techniques, which included filigree, hammering and casting, and an exuberant polychromy of glass paste gems and enamels, made possible pieces with a truly regal impression, despite the low value of the materials used.

This tradition of folk craftsmanship continued well into the nineteenth century, though the effect of the Greek War of Independence (1821-29) was to increase the conscious use of antique motifs that recalled the splendors of classical Greece. The development of Greece as an independent state later in the century led to a slow decline in native folk traditions, but it is very remarkable to realize that an almost unbroken four thousand year old tradition of craftsmanship in precious metals lasted well into modern times.

FIG. 41
*Pectoral ornament
with pendant coins*
NEO-HELLENIC PERIOD

PLATE 80
Bridal diadem
NEO-HELLENIC PERIOD

This type of diadem was originally sewn onto a piece of thick, soft cloth to protect the forehead. It was prized as the most valuable part of bridal attire. The floral symbolism in the decorative designs and rosettes is a very old association between growing plants and human fertility and happiness, as is the pair of confronted birds. The plaque with a female head, now placed in a central position, has close affinities with the old gorgoneion mask, with its power to avert evil.

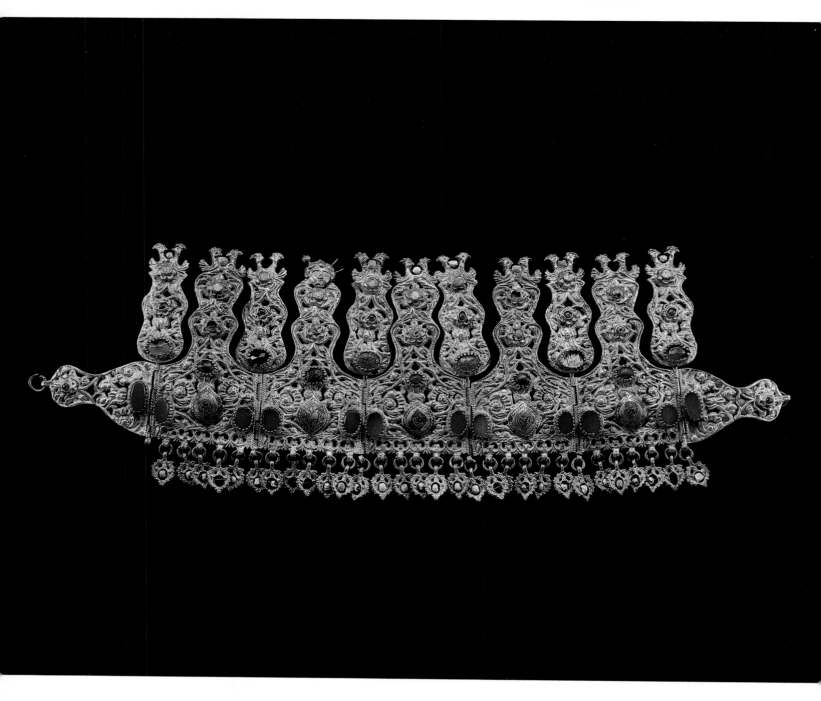

PLATE 81
Enamel belt buckle
Neo-Hellenic Period

Characteristic features of the northern Greek buckle from Thrace are the inscription giving the name of the bridegroom to be, who had the buckle made for his bride, and the date of the engagement, in this case, 1798. This buckle is the end product of a long evolution; fine floral ornaments in gilt wire filigree on a ground of blue, green and black enamel recall 18th-century work, while the rectangular panels and the borders are more medieval in taste.

PLATE 82
Belt buckle
Neo-Hellenic Period

This remarkably large buckle is composed of two discs with cusps like ivy leaves and a stylized pomegranate section between them. Unusual and distinctive ornamentation, especially a profusion of ribbed corals, is characteristic of jewelry thought to have come from Saframpolis in the Pontus region of Asia Minor. This affluent Greek community, near Trebizond on the Black Sea, lasted until the expulsion of Greek-speaking peoples from Turkey in 1922. At that time, this piece and similar ornaments were brought to Greece as family heirlooms.

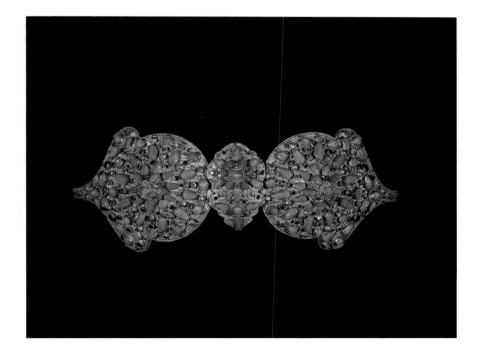

PLATE 83
Frontlet
Neo-Hellenic Period

Such a delicate forehead ornament, composed of cast figure-of-eight segments on either side of a central plaque ornamented with filigree, appliqué strips of gold foil, a drop-shaped coral and a red glass gem, must originally have been attached to a cloth backing. Hanging from the upper ornaments are dangle chains with clusters of coral beads, with longer chains at intervals and even longer ones at the end. This is another example of the Saframpolis style of jewelry. At one edge of the frontlet is a blue glass serpent, a charm against the evil eye.

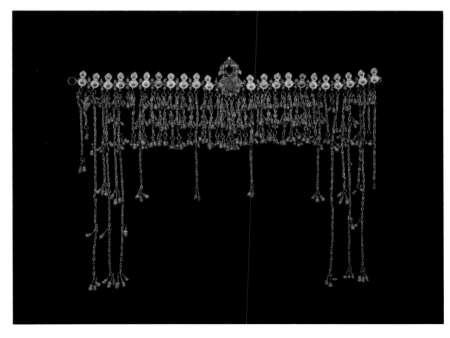

PLATE 84
Pendant
NEO-HELLENIC PERIOD

The earlier part of this pectoral
ornament is the back side with
a cross, together with part
of the side walls. This very
carefully worked material is
Byzantine in date and was
apparently preserved as a
valuable religious relic. In
the 19th century, a filigree
frame with a miniature icon
of the Virgin and a chain
were added to the piece.
This later work was rather
crudely and naively executed
in a Westernized style.

PLATE 85
Bridal pectoral ornament
NEO-HELLENIC PERIOD

Such a bridal ornament, called a *kordoni*, accompanied the bridal costume of village girls from Attica, the farming country around the city of Athens. It was worn over a beaded net-ornament. The size and costliness of the *kordoni* were status symbols, attesting to the wealth and standing of both the bride and bridegroom. Relatives loaded the chains with coins, making up the bride's dowry. After Greek Independence, however, real coins were used for more profitable commercial purposes, and the *kordoni* used imitation coins, as in this example. The filigree rosettes were made by casting in a mold, another sign of a shift away from laborious handicrafts in the late 19th century.

CHECKLIST

NOTE: The numbers in parentheses represent the inventory numbers of the Benaki Museum's permanent collection.

CHAPTER I: THE MYCENAEAN PERIOD

FIG. 1 (2069, 2069a)
Lily-shaped necklace beads
Mycenaean, late Helladic II-IIIA: 15th-14th century B.C.
Gold foil
Thebes
No. 2069: length 0.6 cm, width 1 cm, thickness 0.2 cm, total length of necklace section 18.5 cm
No. 2069a: length 0.7 cm, width 1.013 cm, thickness 0.2 cm, total length of necklace section 2.7 cm

FIG. 2 (2082)
Lentoid seal
Mycenaean, late Helladic IIB-IIIA: 2nd half 15th-14th century B.C.
Carnelian
Thebes
Diameter 2.6-2.7 cm, thickness 1.15 cm

FIG. 3 (7829)
Necklace of semi-precious stones
Mycenaean, late Helladic II-IIIA: 15th-14th century B.C.
Carnelian, rock crystal, amethyst
Provenance unknown
Overall length 24.5 cm

FIG. 4 (2078)
Ring with plain bezel
Mycenaean, late Helladic IIB-IIIA: 2nd half of the 15th-14th century B.C.
Gold
Thebes
Length of bezel 3.6 cm, width of bezel 2.3 cm, diameter of hoop ca. 2 cm

FIG. 5 (2076)
Ring with cloisonné bezel
Mycenaean, late Helladic IIB-IIIA: late 15th-early 14th century, B.C.
Gold
Thebes
Length of bezel 2.6 cm, width 1.9 cm, diameter of hoop ca. 2 cm

PLATE 1 (2068)
Necklace of 32 papyrus-lily shaped beads
Mycenaean, late Helladic IIB-IIIA: 2nd half of the 15th-early 14th century B.C.
Gold foil
Thebes
Total length of necklace 44 cm

PLATE 2 (2070, 2073)
No. 2070: *Pendant in shape of figure-of-eight shield*
Mycenaean, late Helladic II-IIIA: 15th-14th century B.C.
No. 2073: *Pendant in shape of lioness*
Mycenaean, late Helladic II-IIIA: 15th-early 14th century B.C.
Gold foil
Thebes
No. 2070: length 2.9 cm, maximum width 1.95 cm, maximum thickness 1.82 cm
No. 2073: length 1.6 cm, maximum width 0.6 cm, height 0.7 cm

PLATE 3 (2063-2067)
Five rosette appliqués
Mycenaean, late Helladic II-IIIA: 15th-14th century B.C.
Gold foil, repoussé
Thebes
Diameter 5.8 cm

PLATE 4 (2075)
Signet ring with engraving of religious scene
Mycenaean, late Helladic IIB-IIIA: 2nd half of 15th-14th century B.C.
Gold
Thebes
Bezel: length 1.8 cm, width 1.1 cm, diameter of hoop 1.2-1.3 cm

PLATE 5 (2079)
Signet ring with couchant bull
Mycenaean, late Helladic II-IIIA: 15th-early 14th century B.C.
Gold, with bronze core in the hoop
Thebes
Bezel: length 2.7 cm, width 1.6 cm, diameter of hoop 1.8 cm

PLATE 6 (2080)
Cylinder-seal
Mycenaean, late Helladic II-IIIA(?): 15th-14th century B.C.
Gold
Thebes
Height 2.05 cm, diameter 0.9 cm

PLATE 7 (1519)
Pair of earrings in form of bull's head
Cypriot, late Cypriot IIB-IIIA: ca. 1300-1190 B.C.
Sheet gold and gold wire
Provenance unknown
Height 3.2 cm, maximum thickness 0.8 cm, maximum width 1.7 cm

CHAPTER II: FROM GEOMETRIC TO ARCHAIC GREECE

FIG. 6 (2086)
Bull's head pendant
Archaic: 6th-early 5th century B.C.
Gold, decorated in granulation and enamel
Possibly from Thessaly
Height 3.5 cm, width 2.3 cm

FIG. 7 (7884, 7875, 7872, 7886, 7871)
Group of five amulets
Archaic: 750-600 B.C.
Bronze
Macedonia
No. 7884: height 9.1 cm
No. 7875: height 6 cm
No. 7872: height 7.9 cm
No. 7886: height 5.3 cm
No. 7871: height 5.5 cm

FIG. 8 (7896)
Pin
Peloponnesian, Geometric: 850-700 B.C.
Cast bronze with separate disc
Titov Veles
Length 51 cm

Fig. 9 (1526)
Vase-shaped pendant
Archaic: late 6th century B.C.
Gold
Provenance unknown
Height 2.4 cm

Fig. 10 (1525)
Necklace
Archaic: mid-6th century B.C.
Electrum
Provenance unknown
Length 20 cm

Plate 8 (7962)
Spectacle fibula
Macedonian Iron Age: 10th-8th century B.C.
Bronze wire
Macedonia
Length 20 cm, diameter of spiral 8.3 cm

Plate 9 (6242)
Diadem
Orientalizing: 2nd half of 7th century B.C.
Gold
Kos
Length 22.8 cm, height 1.7 cm

Plate 10 (27513)
Gorgoneion
Mid-6th century B.C.
Gold foil
Provenance unknown
Maximum diameter 8.8 cm
Donated by Imre Somlyan

Plate 11 (1532)
Pair of boat earrings
Archaic: late 6th century B.C.
Gold
Provenance unknown
Height 2.3 cm

Plate 12, a-b (3756, 3757)
Pair of sphinxes
Archaic: 6th-5th century B.C.
Gold
Provenance unknown
No. 3756: height 5 cm, length 3.1 cm, thickness of base
 0.7 cm
No. 3757: height 4.5 cm, length 2 cm, thickness of base
 1 cm

Plate 13 (27514)
Ring with kneeling archer on bezel
Late Archaic
Gold
Provenance unknown
Diameter 1.5 cm, diameter of bezel 2.3 cm
Donated by Imre Somlyan

Chapter III: THE CLASSICAL AGE

Fig. 11 (2053)
Bracelet with ram heads (fragmentary)
Classical: late 5th-early 4th century B.C.
Gold, ivory
Provenance unknown
Length 2.6 cm, and 2.7 cm

Fig. 12 (30207)
Pair of bow fibulae
Classical: 1st half of the 5th century B.C.
Silver
Provenance unknown
Length 3.8 cm, 4.5 cm
Donated by George Pappas

Fig. 13 (8136, 8137)
Two bow fibulae
Classical: 1st half of 5th century B.C.
Silver
Chalcidice, Macedonia
Length 3.6 cm, 5.3 cm

Fig. 14 (30005)
Bow fibula
Classical: 4th century B.C.
Gold
Provenance unknown, probably northern Greece
Length 4.5 cm
Donated by George Pappas

Fig. 15 (1567)
Necklace of gold beads
Classical: 4th century B.C.
Gold
Provenance unknown
Length 62 cm

Plate 14 (8119, 8120)
Pair of snake head bracelets
Classical: 1st half of the 5th century B.C.
Silver
Chalcidice, Macedonia
Diameter 3.8 cm, 4 cm

Plate 15 (2053)
Bracelet with ram heads (fragmentary)
Classical: late 5th-early 4th century B.C.
Gold, ivory
Provenance unknown
Length 2.6 cm and 2.7 cm

Plate 16 (1573)
Earring with pyramidal pendant
Classical: 1st half of the 4th century B.C.
Gold
Provenance unknown
Height 3.5 cm

Plate 17 (1541)
Earring with vase-shaped pendant
Classical: 4th century B.C.
Gold
Cyprus
Height 3.6 cm

Plate 18 (8251, 8252)
Pair of bow fibulae
Classical: 4th century B.C.
Gold
Provenance unknown, probably Northern Greece
Length 10.2 cm, 5.3 cm

Plate 19 (1533)
Pair of spiral ornaments
Classical: 4th century B.C.
Bronze with gold foil
The necropolis of Marion-Arsinoe, Cyprus
Length 3.6 cm, diameter 0.4 cm

Plate 20 (2087)
Vase pendant
Greek Classical: 4th century B.C.
Gold
Provenance unknown
Height 2.7 cm, diameter 1.05 cm

Plate 21 (3742)
Bracelet with rams heads
Classical: 4th century B.C.
Gold with filigree and granulation
Provenance unknown
Diameter 8 cm, diameter of tubular hoop 1 cm
(Two views)

Chapter IV: Hellenistic Kingdoms

Fig. 16 (1555)
Torque with lynx-head finials
Hellenistic: 2nd century B.C.
Gold with filigree and garnets
Thessaly
Diameter of torque 12 cm, diameter of tube 1.75 cm

Fig. 17 (1593)
Pair of earrings with bull heads
Hellenistic: 2nd century B.C.
Gold
Provenance unknown (ex-Antoniades Collection)
Diameter 3.5 cm

Fig. 18 (1554)
Necklace with rows of pendants
Hellenistic: 2nd century B.C.
Gold with granulation, garnets, and green enamel
Thessaly
Length 35 cm

Fig. 19 (1561)
Part of necklace
Hellenistic: 1st century B.C.
Gold, garnet, amethyst, emerald, pearls, agate, glass, calcite
Provenance unknown
Length 16 cm

Fig. 20 (1576)
Pair of earrings with doves
Hellenistic: 1st half of 2nd century B.C.
Gold, glass paste
Provenance unknown
Height 4.3 cm

Fig. 21 (1579)
Pair of earrings with erotes
Early Hellenistic
Gold
Provenance unknown
Height 3.4 cm

Plate 22 (2100)
Pair of earrings with vase-shaped pendants
Early Hellenistic: late 4th century B.C.
Gold, green glass paste
Provenance unknown
Height 7 cm

Plate 23 (2092)
Bracelet with rams heads
Hellenistic: late 4th century B.C.
Gold
Provenance unknown
Diameter 8.8 cm

Plate 24 (1578)
Pair of earrings with erotes
Early Hellenistic: late 4th century B.C.
Gold
Provenance unknown (ex-Antoniades Collection)
Height 3.5 cm

Plate 25 (2101)
Pair of earrings with lyre-player
Early Hellenistic: late 4th century B.C.
Gold
Provenance unknown
Height 5.1 cm

Plate 26 (1594)
Pair of earrings with antelope heads
Early Hellenistic
Gold
Provenance unknown
Diameter 3.5 cm

Plate 27 (1597)
Pair of earrings with lion griffin protomes
Early Hellenistic
Gold, glass paste
Provenance unknown
Diameter 3.7 cm

Plate 28 (2062)
Pin with figure of Aphrodite
Hellenistic: 3rd century B.C.
Gold with chalcedony
Provenance unknown
Height 16 cm

Plate 29 (1548, 1549)
Two diadems
Hellenistic: 2nd century B.C.
No. 1548: Gold with garnet, carnelian, green and blue
      enamel, and glass
No. 1549: Gold with carnelian, garnet, and blue and
      white enamel
Thessaly
Height 5 cm, length 23 cm

Plate 30 (1556)
Medallion with bust of Athena
Hellenistic: 2nd century B.C.
Gold with garnet and blue enamel
Thessaly
Diameter 11.1 cm

Plate 31 (1557)
Loutrophoros earring
Hellenistic: 2nd century B.C. (?)
Gold and paste
Thessaly
Height 9 cm

Plate 32 (1551)
Ring with carnelian intaglio of Nike
Hellenistic: early 2nd century B.C.
Gold, carnelian
Thessaly
Bezel: 4 x 3 cm

Plate 33 (1612)
Ring with intaglio bezel
Hellenistic: 2nd century B.C. or later
Gold intaglio
Thessaly
Height (of bezel) 2.2 cm

Plate 34 (1577)
Pair of earrings with carnelian doves
Hellenistic: 2nd century B.C.
Gold, carnelian, jasper
Apulia (ex-Guilhou Collection)
Height 2.8 cm

Plate 35 (1750)
Medallion with bust of Aphrodite
Hellenistic: 2nd century B.C.
Gold, garnet, glass
Alexandria (ex-Antoniades Collection)
Height including loop 3.3 cm

Plate 36 (1563)
Pair of earrings with erotes and masks
Hellenistic: 1st century B.C.
Gold, emerald, garnet, pearls
Provenance unknown
Height 4.35 cm

Plate 37 (1562)
Pair of erotes earrings with Isis crown
Hellenistic: 1st century B.C.
Gold, garnet, emerald
Provenance unknown
Height 6.85 cm (pendant), diameter 29 cm (chain)

PLATE 38 (1560)
Medallion with Eros
Hellenistic: 1st century B.C.
Gold
Provenance unknown, from a former collection in Kertch
Height 5 cm

PLATE 39 (1698)
Snake ring with colored stone medallions
Hellenistic: 1st century B.C.
Gold, carnelian, emerald
Provenance unknown
Diameter 2.4 cm

PLATE 40 (1722, 1723)
Pair of bracelets
Hellenistic period
Silver-gilt foil with incised and punched decoration
Alexandria
No. 1722: Diameter of larger coil 6.4 cm, diameter of smaller coil 6 cm, maximum thickness of foil 0.15 cm
No. 1723: Diameter of each coil 6 cm, maximum thickness of foil 0.15 cm

CHAPTER V: THE ROMAN PERIOD

FIG. 22 (3762)
Oak wreath
Late Hellenistic or Roman
Gold
Provenance unknown (Attica?)
Diameter 14 cm

FIG. 23 (1712)
Snake bracelet
Roman: 1st century A.D.
Gold
Provenance unknown (ex-Antoniades Collection)
Diameter 8.75 cm

FIG. 24 (1632)
Bracelet
Roman: early 1st century A.D.
Gold, emerald
From the Piraeus Grave
Diameter 7.1 cm

FIG. 25 (1737)
Bracelet
Roman: 3rd century A.D.
Gold, sardonyx
Provenance unknown
Diameter 6.5 cm

FIG. 26 (1629)
Garnet ring with intaglio of horseman and foe
Roman: 1st century A.D.
Gold, garnet
From the Piraeus Grave
Height 2.4 cm, width 2.9 cm

PLATE 41 (2061)
Ivy wreath
Late Hellenistic or Roman
Gold
Provenance unknown (Macedonia?)
Diameter 25 cm

PLATE 42 (1674)
Snake ring
Roman: late 1st century B.C.-1st century A.D.
Gold
Provenance unknown
Height 3.8 cm

PLATE 43 (1720, 1721)
Pair of bracelets with Isis and Serapis
Roman: 1st century A.D.
Gold
Provenance unknown(?)
Height (of each) 2.8 cm, diameter 6.1 cm

PLATE 44 (1618-1622)
Set of gold pendants for a necklace
Roman: 1st century A.D.
Gold with colored stones and pearls
Piraeus
Height of *Kantharoi* 4.7 cm, of *lagynoi* 3.5 cm, of *kalathos* 4.2 cm

PLATE 45 (1624-1628)
Amulets: a shell, duck, tortoise, and two fish
Roman: 1st century A.D.
Rock crystal
Pireaus
Lengths: shell 3.3 cm, duck 3.9 cm, tortoise 2.8 cm, each fish 4 cm

PLATE 46 (1631)
Snake head bracelet
Roman: 1st century A.D.
Gold
From the Piraeus Grave
Diameter 11.1 cm

PLATE 47 (2091)
Ring with engraved agate
Roman: 1st-2nd century A.D.
Gold with agate in intaglio
Provenance unknown
Diameter 3.5 cm

PLATE 48 (1636)
Necklace with Medusa medallion and bust of Isis
Roman: 2nd century A.D.
Gold
Provenance unknown
Length 30 cm, diameter of medallion 3.6 cm, height of Isis bust 2.2 cm

PLATE 49 (1744, 1745)
Pair of bracelets
Roman: 3rd century A.D.
Gold
Provenance unknown
No. 1744: Maximum diameter 7.5 cm
No. 1745: Maximum diameter 7.3 cm

PLATE 50 (1640)
Chain with pendant
Roman: 3rd century A.D.
Gold
Provenance unknown
Length chain 31 cm

PLATE 51 (11494)
Bracelet
Roman: 3rd century A.D.
Silver
Provenance unknown
Diameter 7.5 cm

CHAPTER VI: THE EARLY BYZANTINE EMPIRE

FIG. 27 (1672)
Pair of earrings
Byzantine: 4th century A.D.
Gold, glass paste, emerald and carnelian
Provenance unknown
Height 3.6 cm

FIG. 28 (1810)
Pair of earrings
Byzantine: 7th century A.D.
Gold
Provenance unknown
Height 4.4 cm

FIG. 29 (1807)
Pair of earrings
Byzantine: late 5th-early 6th century A.D.
Gold, sapphire, pearls, colored glass
Provenance unknown
Height 9.7 cm

FIG. 30 (1830)
Ring
Byzantine: 6th-7th century A.D.
Gold, niello
Provenance unknown
Diameter 1.6 cm

PLATE 52 (1795/1,2,3)
Sections of a necklace
Byzantine: 5th century A.D.
Gold, precious stones, pearls
Provenance unknown(?)
Height 5.1 - 5.8 cm

PLATE 53 (1778)
Necklace
Byzantine: 5th century A.D.
Gold with sapphires, amethysts, emeralds and pearls
Antinoe, Egypt
Length 42.8 cm

PLATE 54 (1835-1836)
Pair of bracelets
Byzantine: 6th century A.D.
Gold
Cyprus (?)
Diameter 8.8 cm

PLATE 55 (1837)
Bracelet clasp
Byzantine: late 6th century A.D.
Gold and niello
Provenance unknown(?)
Height 1.4 cm, width 3.7 cm

PLATE 56 (1829)
Ring
Byzantine: 6th-7th century A.D.
Gold
Provenance unknown(?)
Diameter 2.5 cm

PLATE 57 (1826)
Ring
Byzantine: 6th-7th century A.D.
Gold
Provenance unknown(?)
Height 2.9 cm

PLATE 58 (2107)
Swivel ring
Byzantine: 6th-7th century A.D.
Gold
Provenance unknown
Diameter 2.1 cm, thickness 0.2 - 0.35 cm

PLATE 59 (1849)
Cross
Byzantine: early 7th century A.D.
Gold
Provenance unknown(?)
Height 3 cm

PLATE 60 (11437)
Buckle and belt plate
Byzantine: 6th century A.D.
Silver
Provenance unknown(?)
Length 7.3 cm, width 3.2 cm, height 1.2 cm

CHAPTER VII: THE LATER BYZANTINE EMPIRE

FIG. 31 (11438a)
Reliquary cross
Byzantine: 9th-10th centuries
Silver, niello
Provenance unknown
Height 7.3 cm, width 4.4 cm, thickness 1 cm

FIG. 32 (11438b)
Reliquary cross with inner cross
Byzantine: 9th-10th centuries
Silver, niello
Provenance unknown
Height 7.3 cm, width 4.4 cm, thickness 1 cm

FIG. 33 (8837)
Oval plaque with hinge/suspension-lugs
Byzantine: 10th-11th century A.D.
Gold cloisonné enamel
Provenance unknown
Height (overall) 29.9 mm, height (oval) 26.4 mm, width 22.45 mm, thickness 4.45 mm

FIG. 34 (1853)
Pectoral cross (back view)
Byzantine: 13th-14th century A.D.
Gold and lapis lazuli
Provenance unknown
Height 4 cm, thickness 0.7 cm

PLATE 61 (21992, 21993, 21994)
Reliquary crosses
Byzantine: 11th century A.D.
Silver, niello
Provenance unknown(?)
Height 7.1 cm, width 3.5 cm
Donated by Helen Stathatos

PLATE 62 (11457)
Bracelet
Byzantine: 11th century A.D.
Silver (partially gilded), niello
Provenance unknown(?)
Height 3.3 cm, diameter 5.5 cm

PLATE 63 (11436)
Medusa amulet (back view)
Byzantine: 12th century A.D.
Silver
Provenance unknown(?)
Diameter 6.6 cm, thickness 0.2 cm

PLATE 64 (11436)
Medusa amulet (front view)
Byzantine: 12th century A.D.
Silver
Provenance unknown(?)
Diameter 6.6 cm, thickness 0.2 cm

PLATE 65 (2113)
Encolpium
Byzantine: 12th century A.D. in a 16th-century mount
Rock crystal, silver-gilt, precious stones, pearls
Provenance unknown(?)
Height 6 cm, thickness 1.2 cm

PLATE 66 (1820)
Earring
Byzantine: 12th century A.D.
Gold
Provenance unknown(?)
Height 5.3 cm

PLATE 67 (1853)
Pectoral cross
Byzantine: 13th-14th century A.D.
Gold and lapis lazuli
Provenance unknown(?)
Height 4 cm, thickness 0.7 cm

CHAPTER VIII: POST-BYZANTINE GREECE

FIG. 35 (7669)
Pectoral in the shape of a four-masted sailing boat
Post-Byzantine period: 1st half of the 17th century
Gold with polychrome filigree enamel and pearls
Island of Patmos
Length 13.8 cm, width 9.5 cm
Donated by Helen A. Stathatos

FIG. 36 (Ea 711)
Head ornament with chains and pendants
Post-Byzantine period: late 17th-early 18th century A.D.
Cast silver, gilded details, granulation, glass gems
Northern Macedonia
Height 24 cm, width 29.5 cm

FIG. 37 (1987)
Pendant (back view)
Post-Byzantine period: 2nd half of the 17th century A.D.
Gold, silver-gilt, chalcedony, emeralds, enamel
Constantinople
Height 4.8 cm

FIG. 38 (1987)
Pendant (front view)
Post-Byzantine period: 2nd half of the 17th century A.D.
Gold, silver-gilt, chalcedony, emeralds, enamel
Constantinople
Height 4.8 cm

PLATE 68 (1799)
Pendant
Post-Byzantine period: 1580
Gold, agate, amethyst, enamel
Provenance unknown
Diameter 10.3 cm
Donated by Alexandre Choremi-Benaki

PLATE 69 (7670)
Earrings with pendants in the form of three-masted caravels
Post-Byzantine period: Mid-17th century
Gold with polychrome filigree enamel and pearls
From the island of Siphnos
Length 12.4 cm, width 5.9 cm
Donated by Helen Stathatos

PLATE 70 (Exp 601)
*Necklace of lozenge-shaped segments with a
    pear-shaped pendant*
Post-Byzantine period: Mid-18th century A.D.
Gold with polychrome filigree enamel and miniatures
    on paper
From the island of Patmos
Length 33.5 cm

PLATE 71 (Exp 265)
"Dangle" earrings with bell-shaped pendants
Post Byzantine period: 2nd half of the 18th century A.D.
Openwork gold foil with filigree decoration and seed pearls
From the island of Kos in the Dodecanese
Length 20.5 cm

PLATE 72 (1517)
Three pendants from a pectoral ornament
Post-Byzantine period: 18th-early 19th century A.D.
Gold filigree and pearls
From the island of Corfu
a) height 14.5 cm; maximum width 6.5 cm
b) height 13.5 cm; maximum width 6.5 cm
c) height 13 cm; maximum width 6 cm

PLATE 73 (BE 786)
Torque
Post-Byzantine period: 1691
Cast silver, partly gilt, amethysts, carnelians, green
    glass gems
Macedonia
Diameter 19.5 cm
Held on trust for Epi Protonotariou-Pavlidi, 1989

PLATE 74 (10400a)
Panaghiarion (outside view)
Post-Byzantine period: 1624-1639, 1667-1668
Ivory, silver-gilt, niello
Provenance unknown(?)
Diameter 7.7 cm

PLATE 75 (10400b)
Panaghiarion (inside view)
Post-Byzantine period: 1624-1639, 1667-1668
Ivory, silver-gilt, niello
Provenance unknown(?)
Diameter 7.7 cm

PLATE 76 (7660a)
Ecclesiastical pectoral (obverse)
Post-Byzantine period: late 17th-early 18th century A.D.
Gold, silver-gilt, garnets, emeralds, enamel
Constantinople
Height 6 cm, width 4.7 cm
Presented by Helen Stathatos

PLATE 77 (7660b)
Ecclesiastical pectoral (reverse)
Post-Byzantine period: late 17th-early 18th century A.D.
Gold, silver-gilt, garnets, emeralds, enamel
Constantinople
Height 6 cm, width 4.7 cm
Presented by Helen Stathatos

PLATE 78 (TA 147a)
Pectoral belonging to Metropolitan Parthenios (back view)
Post-Byzantine period: 1738
Gold, rubies, sapphires, emeralds, enamel
Constantinople
Diameter 9 cm
Exchangeable Populations Fund

PLATE 79 (TA147b)
Pectoral belonging to Metropolitan Parthenios (front view)
Post-Byzantine period: 1738
Gold, rubies, sapphires, emeralds, enamel
Constantinople
Diameter 9 cm
Exchangeable Populations Fund

CHAPTER IX: NEO-HELLENIC GREECE

FIG. 39 (Ea 1374)
Belt buckle
Neo-Hellenic: mid-18th century
Silver-gilt, cast, hammered and perforated in places, with
    agates and niello
Epiros
Height 13 cm, width 26 cm

FIG. 40 (Ea 1744)
Silver choker with pendant coins
Neo-Hellenic: 2nd half of the 18th century A.D.
Cast silver, partly gilt, with pierced decoration, granulation,
    enamel, agate, turquoise, corals and glass gems
Macedonia
Diameter 11.5 cm, height of braid 3 cm
Donated by Marina Lappa-Diomidi

FIG. 41 (Ea 2158)
Pectoral ornament with pendant coins
Neo-Hellenic: mid-19th century A.D.
Silver-gilt chains and coins
Tanagra, Boeotia
Height 16 cm, maximum width 42.5 cm (fully stretched)

PLATE 80 (Ea 676)
Bridal diadem
Neo-Hellenic: late 18th century A.D.
Silver-gilt, cast, hammered and perforated, with carnelians,
    corals, turquoise, glass gems and niello
From Pogoni, Epiros
Height 13 cm, width 30 cm

PLATE 81 (Ea 220)
Inscribed enameled belt buckle
Neo-Hellenic: 1798
Silver, gilded details, enamel, corals and glass gems
Thrace
Maximum height 10.5 cm, width 19.5 cm

PLATE 82 (TA 257)
Belt buckle
Neo-Hellenic: 1837
Silver-gilt, filigree, enamel, corals and glass gems
Kermira, Asia Minor
Height 11.5 cm, width 31.5 cm
Exchangeable Populations Fund

PLATE 83 (Ea 1399)
Frontlet
Neo-Hellenic: 1st half of the 19th century A.D.
Cast silver-gilt, filigree, corals, a glass gem
Saframpolis, Pontus (?)
Height 8-22 cm, width 31.5 cm

PLATE 84 (1990)
Pendant
Neo-Hellenic: 19th century (obverse and mounting)
Byzantine: (reverse)
Gold, pearls, paint, cord
Provenance unknown
Height 4.8 cm, thickness 0.9 cm

PLATE 85 (Ea 1275)
Bridal pectoral chain ornament
Neo-Hellenic: 1870-1890
Silver-gilt, cast filigree, glass gems
Attica
Length 59.5 cm